The Deliberate Doctorate

T0274717

The **On Campus** imprint of UBC Press features publications designed for the diverse members of the university community – students, faculty, instructors, staff, and administrators. **On Campus** offers a range of interesting, sometimes unconventional, but always useful information. All **On Campus** works are assessed by experts in the field prior to publication. To ensure affordability, PDFs are available as free downloads from the UBC Press website, with print and other digital formats also available through our website, bookstores, and libraries.

On Campus books are designed to help readers successfully meet the intellectual and social challenges encountered at university or college today and include:

How to Succeed at University (and Get a Great Job!):
Mastering the Critical Skills You Need for School, Work, and Life,
by Thomas R. Klassen and John A. Dwyer
(also available in French from University of Ottawa Press)

It's All Good (Unless It's Not): Mental Health Tips and Self-Care Strategies for Your Undergrad Years, by Nicole Malette

You @ the U: A Guided Tour through Your First Year of University,
by Janet Miller

The Successful TA: A Practical Approach to Effective Teaching,
by Kathy M. Nomme and Carol Pollock

TL;DR: A Very Brief Guide to Reading and Writing in University,
by Joel Heng Hartse

To find out more about **On Campus** books visit www.ubcpress.ca.

Leela
Viswanathan

The
Deliberate
Doctorate
A Values-Focused
Journey to Your
PhD

UBC PRESS

32 31 30 29 28 27 26 25 24 23   5 4 3 2 1

Printed in Canada on FSC-certified ancient-forest-free paper (100% post-consumer recycled) that is processed chlorine- and acid-free.

Library and Archives Canada Cataloguing in Publication
Title: The deliberate doctorate : a values-focused journey to your PhD / Leela Viswanathan.
Names: Viswanathan, Leela, author.
Description: Includes bibliographical references.
Identifiers: Canadiana (print) 20230229433 | Canadiana (ebook) 20230229492
ISBN 9780774839112 (softcover) | ISBN 9780774839136 (EPUB)
ISBN 9780774839129 (PDF)
Subjects: LCSH: Doctor of philosophy degree. | LCSH: Doctoral students.
Classification: LCC LB2386 .V57 2023 | DDC 378.2—dc23

UBC Press gratefully acknowledges the financial support for our publishing program of the Government of Canada (through the Canada Book Fund), the Canada Council for the Arts, and the British Columbia Arts Council.

Printed and bound in Canada by Friesens
Set in New Caledonia and Tw Cen MT by Gerilee McBride
Copy editor: Lesley Erickson
Cover designer: Gerilee McBride

UBC Press
The University of British Columbia
2029 West Mall
Vancouver, BC V6T 1Z2
www.ubcpress.ca

To Amma and Appa,
for loving me into being.

Contents

Figures and Tables   viii

Acknowledgments   ix

Introduction Being Deliberate   5

1 Discovering Your Values   15

2 Setting Goals Aligned with Your Values   31

3 Making the Most of Your PhD Supervisor   47

4 Assembling Your Supervisory Team   63

5 Networking without Feeling Smarmy about It   77

6 "Feeling All the Feels" through Your PhD   93

7 Defining Success on Your Own Terms   109

Conclusion Living Your Values   121

Further Reading   125

Figures

My Universe of Possibilities / 2–3
My Values / 19
Domain, My Goals, and My Activities / 45
My Resources / 61
My People / 75
Three Circles of People to Build Your Network / 78
My Network / 91
What Success Means to Me / 118

Tables

The Skills Inventory / 37–40
Charting Your Wishes / 66–67

Acknowledgments

THIS BOOK WAS LOVED into being with the support, encouragement, and expertise of many people.

Thanks to the students, teachers, colleagues, and employers I've had the honour and the opportunity to work with over the years. The time I spent learning from you inspired this book.

To Nadine Pedersen at On Campus: Thank you for your consistent editorial support and for encouraging me to bring my heart and my head to this project. You prove that there are creative people in publishing who can offer support and guidance on sharing stories in an accessible, nonexploitative manner.

To James MacNevin at UBC Press: Thanks for believing in me and connecting me with Nadine.

To Kristin Agnello, Alana Butler, Erin Clow, Liette Gilbert, Sheena Jardine-Olade, Sarah Minnes, Heidi Penning, Rebecca Pero, Ramneek K. Pooni, and Sheila Stewart: Thanks for informing this manuscript at various stages of development and for helping me find ways to make it practical and informative while being true to myself.

To Shyra and Rye Barberstock, Ellyn Clost-Lambert, Andrea Hiltz, Kathy Hoover, Sarah Knight, the Minnes Family, Beverley Mullings, the Monday Night De-Stress Group, Ramya Raghavan, Rebecca Tan, and Mona L. Warner: Your brilliance and kindness uplifted my health and well-being.

To Meena Viswanathan, my dear Akka: In my changing universe of possibilities, I feel so fortunate that you remain my constant ally and most ardent supporter.

I'm especially grateful for the editorial insights of Iva Cheung and Lesley Erickson, and for the thoughtful input of the anonymous external readers. Any errors and omissions are my own.

The Deliberate Doctorate

Domain: _____

My People

A M S

_____ [ ] [ ] [ ]

_____ [ ] [ ] [ ]

_____ [ ] [ ] [ ]

_____ [ ] [ ] [ ]

My Activities

_____

_____

_____

My Goals

1 _____

2 _____

3 _____

Names of people in my inner circle

_____

_____

_____

_____

Names of people in my middle circle

_____

_____

_____

_____

Names of people in my outer circle

_____

_____

_____

_____

My Goals

1 _____

2 _____

3 _____

My People

A M S

_____ [ ] [ ] [ ]

_____ [ ] [ ] [ ]

_____ [ ] [ ] [ ]

_____ [ ] [ ] [ ]

My Activities

_____

_____

_____

Domain: _____

My Universe of Possibilities

Date: _____

My People

A M S

[ ] [ ] [ ]

[ ] [ ] [ ]

[ ] [ ] [ ]

[ ] [ ] [ ]

My Activities

_____

_____

_____

My Goals

1 _____

2 _____

3 _____

My Values

1 _____

2 _____

3 _____

4 _____

5 _____

Domain: _____

My Resources

_____

_____

_____

_____

_____

What Success Means to Me

_____

_____

A printable version of this map is available at ubcpress.ca/the-deliberate-doctorate.

Introduction

Being Deliberate

I CONSIDERED APPLYING to do a PhD three times. The first time I applied, I was twenty-eight years old. I had a job as a planner, but it was precarious. Just two years before, I'd graduated with a master's degree in planning, and I was already disillusioned about my career prospects. So after careful consideration of a PhD in planning, I applied to a university in the United States. Although I had secured a supervisor, my application was rejected. The department had no funding for Canadians and other international students. I was disappointed by the outcome; however, I was also averse to incurring debt, so I returned to my job search.

Two years later, when I was thirty, my work contract was coming to an end. I decided to search for a career-advancing job and investigate PhD programs in planning and policy. I encountered a PhD coordinator who spoke disparagingly about my four years spent outside of academia. They questioned my capacity to succeed in a PhD program. Their words brought an end to my inquiries and triggered self-doubt. I gave up, maybe too easily. However, I eventually landed a permanent job as a government policy adviser.

In retrospect, these first two attempts at applying to programs were rooted in my desire to escape boredom and precarious work situations. I lacked guidance. And my reasons for pursuing a doctorate were not well thought out. Instead of exploring, with curiosity, what I valued – what I *really* wanted – I had reverted to the familiar.

My third attempt at applying to a PhD program, in March and April 2002, was inspired by two significant events in my volunteer and professional policy work. The first took place while volunteering in Toronto as a drop-in mentor to youth who, like me, traced their ancestry to a country in South Asia (i.e., Bangladesh, Bhutan, India, Pakistan, Nepal, or Sri Lanka). During one of our group talks, some of the youth shared that they saw no point in going to university. They explained that their parents, who had engineering or accounting degrees from India or Pakistan, were making their living driving taxis and delivering pizzas. The youth debated the merits of going to university if "driving and delivery" were the ultimate outcomes of a university education. I explained that their lives could turn out quite different from their parents' because they had opportunities their parents had not had as youths. Some reasoned that a university education would improve their prospects, but others remained unconvinced. I shared my intention to apply for a PhD so I could become a more effective researcher, have the time to do thoughtful and informed research, and teach. One of the youths said, "Leela, I would probably go to university if I knew there was someone like you teaching. Someone who cares about me. Someone brown like us." I interpreted their words as a sign. I wanted to become *that* teacher.

A few weeks later, I experienced the second significant event. As a policy adviser and researcher in the Ontario provincial government, I'd spent six months working on a piece of legislation to remove barriers to work for internationally educated professionals. My colleagues had already contributed three years of work to this effort. My job was to answer content-related questions raised by the team of lawyers writing the legislation. I enjoyed using my research skills, checking facts, and talking to the lawyers in lay terms about the intentions of policy. On the last day of the project, a momentous twelve-hour day, one of the lawyers explained that the draft legislation would be printed on purple paper, a shade symbolic of royalty. The draft legislation was then submitted to cabinet for final reading and approval –

the final step before the draft legislation would become provincial law. When I went home that night, I felt good about my contributions. Not even rumours of a cabinet shuffle dampened my spirits. But the next morning the rumours were confirmed. The Ontario provincial cabinet, under Ernie Eves, was reshuffled; this overhaul could shift policy priorities and disrupt the legislative process. Legislation might be put on hold, or even worse, sent to the chopping block. Fortunately, "my" minister was not part of the cabinet reshuffle, so I remained optimistic as I rode the elevator to my office. When I stepped out, I found the corridor flanked on both sides by transparent plastic bags full of shredded purple paper! In that moment, I knew all my efforts to do credible research, to offer valuable advice, and to change the lives of internationally educated professionals would amount to nothing. A few hours later, when it was confirmed that the government's priorities had shifted and our proposed legislation was not going forward, my decision to follow through on my PhD application was cemented.

These two significant events showed me that I wanted to be a teacher, that I wanted to make a difference in the lives of students who didn't see themselves represented in academia. I wanted to train as an academic researcher so I'd have more credibility and influence. After reflecting on my values, I completed my application. I identified people in my network who could help me align my values with my goals. I might not have needed a PhD to achieve these goals, but what I also found out about myself was that I wanted prestige, accountability, research experience, and more time to reflect on and construct ideas rather than simply react to them.

Despite this realization, my admission process was still bumpy. I applied to the program I felt would best help me achieve my goals and uphold my values. I was interviewed on more than one occasion and asked questions about why, as a thirty-four-year-old "mature student," I wanted to get a PhD? I persevered and was admitted into the environmental studies program at York University, in Toronto, in fall 2002. I was thirty-nine years old when I graduated and took up a two-year teaching and research postdoctoral fellowship at Queen's University in Kingston. After that, I worked as a tenure-track professor at Queen's for six years and achieved tenure (a.k.a. landed a job for life) in 2015. Four years later, in 2019, seeing that my values no longer aligned with my aspirations within academia, I left my associate professor position and launched my own consulting company. My journey continues.

Why Read This Book?

I wrote this book to guide students who are trying to decide whether to pursue a PhD. It's a big life decision because it has a long-term impact on more than one life sphere (e.g., education, career, finances, work-life balance, relationships) and requires an investment in self-trust. This book is also for current PhD students who want to be more deliberate in pursuing their path to degree completion and beyond. No matter where you are on the path to earning your PhD, this book offers a guide for keeping your values as your constant touchstone on your journey.

This book also reflects my desire to influence postsecondary education systems and foster environments where students can flourish. But I didn't set out to write a critique of universities. By showing you some of the imperfections of university systems, I encourage you to forge your own path as a PhD student and gain the support you need to succeed on your own terms. I show you how to offer support to your peers in a manner that doesn't perpetuate toxic practices that all too often feed student burnout. Collective wellness and your success as a student need not be mutually exclusive. You can foster an environment of support and wellness as a foundation for growth. I encourage all students to talk to themselves, their supervisors, and others about boundaries and expectations. Anyone who hopes to help graduate students navigate their doctoral programs effectively and mindfully will benefit from this book.

Introduction

This book would not exist if my family hadn't stressed the importance of education. I grew up with what felt like an ancestral obligation to go to university. I'm the daughter of immigrants from India who instilled in me the belief that postsecondary education is a liberatory experience, one that leads to knowledge, skills, and credentials that translate into a higher income, respect for oneself, and prestige in society. My father was the only person in his family to go to university in India. On my mother's side – at a time when girls were groomed mostly, if not solely, for marriage – my maternal grandfather incurred debt to ensure that all four of his daughters went to college. After immigrating to and settling in Canada, my parents eventually earned graduate degrees from McGill. My father earned a PhD in plant pathology before my sister and I were born, and my mother earned an MA in education while caring for us. Although my father died soon after my tenth birthday and my mother raised my sister and me on a fixed income, I did well at school, stayed in my hometown of Montreal, and graduated from McGill with a BA in sociology after switching out of architecture. Buttressed by student loans, I pursued a professional master's degree in planning as a means to get a "good job" and "make a difference." My decision to embark on my PhD journey came with greater deliberation and deeper exploration of my values.

Being from a family that prioritized education, with a mother who had a graduate degree, gave me an advantage over my peers who were first-generation students who had to figure out how to gain admission to and navigate university. At the same time, getting into a program as a mature student was more challenging for me than it may have been if I'd applied following my master's degree as a younger student.

And being a racialized woman in academia, a space that remains predominantly white, has meant that I've had to contend with situations that would be unfamiliar to many, but not all, of my non-racialized peers. For example, I've felt the need to address racial microaggressions and establish my English-speaking Canadian roots when reaching out to new contacts (to reduce the likelihood of being

9

ignored or rejected because of my long South Asian last name and racial biases). But I don't have experience navigating university as an international student who doesn't have my advantages, or as someone with a disability, or as someone who is Indigenous, or as someone who is 2SLGBTQ+.

No matter who you are or what led you to pick up this book, I hope you'll find a point of connection to my stories. I use stories in this book because they're useful ways to explore how your values reflect who you are and who you want to become. I also hope you'll benefit from the exercises, designed to help you stay connected to your values – what matters most to you – during your PhD journey.

My own experiences are based in the context of Canadian universities and the social science disciplines of geography, environmental studies, and urban planning. But you don't have to go to a Canadian university or pursue a degree in the social sciences to learn how to identify your values and make them central to your PhD journey. Values are rooted first and foremost in humanity. Knowing your values can help you make an informed, deliberate decision about whether to start a PhD. Reflecting periodically on what you really want can enable you to take deliberate steps toward earning your doctorate. (Readers seeking reflections on university experiences in Europe or the Americas, or in the STEM disciplines, will find more resources in the Further Reading section.)

The Stages of Your PhD Journey

If you're just starting your PhD or contemplating pursuing a PhD, you should know that there are key stages along the journey and that universities have rites of passage in the form of exams and paperwork to document a student's transition from one stage to the next. In general, there are four stages to the PhD journey: admission, precandidacy, candidacy, and graduation.

Some programs require students to choose and secure a PhD supervisor before admission is granted. Following admission, PhD students may be required to take mandatory and/or optional courses as part of their precandidacy requirements. In the precandidacy stage, the student might also identify their advisory or supervisory team, some-times referred to as a supervisory committee, and if they did not select them prior to admission, they might choose their supervisor too. The supervisor is also a member of the student's supervisory team. A research proposal is crucial. Some programs expect a student to arrive with a proposal in hand, which the student will likely refine with their supervisor. Other programs expect students to write their proposal within the first two years of their studies, either from scratch or based on research their supervisor has under way. In most disciplines, you are not considered a candidate until you pass an exam where you demonstrate "comprehensive" knowledge of your discipline. The exam may also include proposal approval.

Through most of the candidacy phase, candidates conduct and complete their research and synthesize it into a dissertation (ostensibly one big book of your research), a portfolio of articles for peer review and publication, or another type of deliverable, such as research that combines creative practices (e.g., a curated visual art exhibit, theatric performance, or other artistic expression) with a scholarly investigation and written work based on academic research. The dissertation or final series of deliverables is submitted to and often orally defended in the presence of a dissertation committee (often made up of the student's supervisory team members, with one representative external to the student's university and at arm's length from the student's research). If successful, the candidate is awarded their degree and graduates.

Although this book uses a four-year degree completion timeframe in its description of scenarios, you should be aware that each university and PhD program has its own milestones or checkpoints to ensure that students meet their degree requirements within a specified timeframe. I encourage you to familiarize yourself with them. And while some doctoral programs take four years to complete, others can take six years or more. Please refer to the Further Reading section for additional resources that map out the stages of the PhD journey based on systems in the United Kingdom, Canada, and the United States.

How to Use This Book

This book is tied together by a map (My Universe of Possibilities, pages 2–3) to help you summarize the results of the reflection exercises. As you proceed through the chapters, you'll customize the map. Your values are the map's central point of reference. You'll also be prompted to draw connections among the people in your network who can help you keep focused and grounded. The map, when completed, will help you reflect on your values as you pursue your PhD deliberately.

I recommend that you start a journal, real or digital, where you can take notes and jot down ideas and responses that come to you as you do the exercises. To complete the exercises, you might set aside up to an hour a day for three weeks, or you might devote a morning each weekend for five weeks. I encourage you to read the book chapters in the order they appear, as ideas build from one chapter to the next so that you can systematically populate the map. At different moments throughout the book, I'll encourage you to revisit your map and reflect on its contents. The map is also available as a printable PDF at ubcpress.ca/the-deliberate-doctorate.

If you need to take a break from the exercises, feel free to jump ahead to Chapter 6 to reflect on the emotional aspects of the PhD journey. At the end of the book, I'll invite you to revisit your values and consider whether they've shifted priority and, if they have, whether there are new directions you might choose to take. Being deliberate about your choices, aware of the constraints you might face, and open to opportunities in your universe of possibilities will help you thrive during your PhD journey.

This book is organized on the premise that, much like life, the PhD is about the journey, not the destination. The seven chapters are sequenced so that you can deliberate – that is, both reflect and *act* deliberately to connect with your people and navigate through the structural and emotional aspects of your journey.

Chapter 1 shows you how to identify your values and prioritize them. I'll invite you to reflect on who you are and what you want, and you'll place your top five values in the star located at the centre of the map of your universe of possibilities (see pages 2–3). This is a crucial part of the book, the foundation from which all the other exercises will follow. I encourage you to explore the domains of your PhD, such as coursework, research, and professional development, among others, and to consider how activities in each domain could manifest your values. I'll also introduce you to the importance of establishing healthy boundaries.

Chapter 2 shows you how to derive your goals from your values so they're aligned. You'll learn to set goals informally and formally. The chapter's skills inventory will help you assess the skills you bring to your PhD, identify skills you may want to learn or enhance, and list activities that help you practise your values and achieve your goals. At the end of the chapter, you'll be prompted to draw connections among your goals, skills, activities, and values.

Doing a PhD is not a solo journey. After you, your supervisor is the most important person on your path to achieving your doctorate. Chapter 3 equips you with key questions to ask a potential supervisor and with suggestions to manage your relationship with your supervisor. You'll explore mutual expectations with your supervisor as a gateway to examining and identifying values, goals, and resources to put on your map.

Chapter 4 builds on your work in Chapter 3 to help you to assemble a supervisory team. You'll have an opportunity to seek out what you need from the members of your supervisory team and explore their roles as allies, mentors, or sponsors. Based on their knowledge and expertise, your goals, and your skills, you'll consider who among your team can be listed as "My People" in each "Domain" on your map.

Chapter 5 leads you through exercises to identify more of "your people" – the people you want to network with and who can become part of your network. You'll learn how to build a network of people who will populate your inner, middle, and outer circles of supporters. You'll learn how to draw from these circles to engage in conversations – or network – without feeling smarmy about it.

Chapter 6 highlights your agency and worth as a student scholar by exploring the emotional aspects of your PhD journey. This chapter validates the presence and importance of emotions and of working through them. It will prompt you to consider how you might revisit your values during times of personal strife to reconnect to what matters to you most. You'll identify people who will support your wellness and help you break through cycles of stress. You'll also be encouraged to add wellness support to the resources on your map.

Success can mean many things. Chapter 7 encourages you to strategize and define success on your own terms. To do this, you must give yourself the time to build a growth mindset and explore the options that a PhD affords you, before and after graduation. Choosing not to complete a PhD or choosing to pursue a career outside of academia are acceptable options to achieve success on your own terms.

I end with a message that explores the possibilities for you as a PhD student and future graduate. I provide a list of sources for further reading, linked to the content of each chapter. These sources are the starting point for your further deliberation.

Although you may not yet know whether to pursue a PhD or in what direction to take your PhD, I hope that reading this book will help you to find out.

Discovering Your Values

1

VALUES REFLECT WHAT YOU really want. Not in the material sense (like a new bike or a vintage pair of boots) but in terms of how you want to behave – what bell hooks refers to as "habits of being" that link how you think to what you do. Values are what guide and motivate you to act. Values will bring intention to your goal setting as you map the path to your PhD. Discovering your values doesn't have to be complicated, but it can be challenging. This chapter provides you with self-reflection exercises to help you. You'll also learn to set and respect boundaries to help you to practise your values. Knowing your values can provide a touchstone to test your goals and boundaries.

What Are Values?

The word "values" is another way of saying "ways of being true to yourself" or "following your heart's deepest desires." "Morals" and "values" are often used interchangeably because they're both linked to behaviours. But they're different. Morals are rooted in institutional and societal expectations, including processes of socialization and religious, philosophical, and legal frameworks. Values are based on personal principles that motivate a person to live their best life.

Words like "should," "shall," or "must" are statements and judgments. Living according to morals considered to be "good" or "great" by a society might garner you praise or higher social status, whereas living according to morals considered "bad" might lead you to be rejected or marginalized. Morals are considered virtues in Western philosophy, in terms of how they relate to "being good" or to "good citizenship." By contrast, values are deeply personal, and it's often hard to explain why you have them to someone else. Values feel like intuition and may not be obviously rooted in societal or organizational rules and norms. In other words, you may develop values independent of a desire to gain favour with society or another human system, like an organization or faith group. A person can rediscover or reject morals or values they inherited as a child and discover new values over time.

Morals change along with societal norms (i.e., laws of government and the justice system). As you experience life events and transform because of them, your values might also change. Or your values might not change at all; they might shift in priority. For example, independence and financial prosperity are two of my values; however, while independence continues to rank high among my values, financial prosperity has slipped to a medium-low value since the time I was a tenured professor. This baffled me at first, because having money is independence, or at least that's what I learned as a child growing up with a single parent. On deeper reflection, although financial prosperity is important to my needs and desires, and to my current state of independence, it ranks lower because my concept of what is "enough" has changed.

What Are Your Values?

It might feel too hard to answer the question, What do I really want? So here are other questions to consider to discover your values:

- What do I stand for now or want to stand for?
- What holds meaning in my life now?
- What activities bring meaning to my life now? How do these activities make me/others feel?
- What matters to me now? What activities do I do that reflect what matters to me?

    If your mind is drawing a blank when it comes to values, there are lists online to help you get started; they're often labelled as the most common "core values" of human beings.

Here is my list of common values. I've left space for you to add more, as you discover them. Use this list to clarify your values and prioritize them. You may be practising several of these values in more than one sphere of your life. You can use this list for any area in your life (e.g., home life, relationships, caregiving) and for your PhD, and that's why I listed so many of them. Next to each value, you can indicate how important the value is to you at this moment (V = very important; I = important; N = not that important).

A Non-exhaustive List of Common Values

accountability

creativity

achievement

environmental concerns

assertiveness

equity

autonomy / independence

fairness / justice

belonging

financial prosperity

caring for others /
self-care

fitness (physical and mental)

flexibility

connection / ·
being engaged

forgiveness /
self-forgiveness

cooperation

freedom (in how you live
and help others to achieve)

courage

generosity	order / organization
honesty	respect
humility	responsibility
independence	sensuality and pleasure
interdependence	sexuality
intimacy	spirituality
love	trust / trustworthiness / self-trust
loyalty	... and what else?
mental wellness	... and what else?
objectivity	... and what else?

As a reflection exercise, decide which values you consider "very important" and "important." Now, think about the activities you do outside of school (i.e., in the rest of your life) that reflect your most important values. Write down these activities in your journal; they represent activities where you practise your values. Do you engage in those activities often? Would you like to be spending more time on one activity than another? Think about which values you practise in more than one activity and those you practise in just one activity. Your top five values are likely among those you labelled "very important" or "important." Pick your top five values as you prioritized them and place them in the following figure. You'll refer to these values throughout your PhD journey and as you complete the exercises in this book.

My Values

1 _____

2 _____

3 _____

4 _____

5 _____

Now, scan the values you labelled "not important." Take note of them. Maybe you're not engaged in activities where you would practise these values. Maybe these values were once important and are no longer. Can you think of another reason why these values are not important to you (anymore)? There are free values assessments and inventories online that can help you identify values and prioritize them. They will prompt you to explore values you practise in all areas of your life (e.g., work, school, recreation, family). My favourite online values inventory is listed in the Further Reading section. Online values assessments let you identify and prioritize your values efficiently. I also highly recommend sitting quietly by yourself or going for a walk in nature or your favourite urban jungle and listening to what your heart desires – your values will emerge.

Your PhD's Domains

As you discover how your values are prioritized, I encourage you to consider the different domains of your PhD. Your domains might include coursework, research lab work, professional development, or other areas. Then consider how each domain could manifest some of your "very important" values; you can do this by considering activities in each domain. Look at your top five values, and in your notebook jot down activities that you might be doing, or would like to do, to practise your values in your PhD program. Add these activities to your list of activities where you practise your values in the rest of your life. For now, just hold on to your list of activities; you'll review them again in Chapter 2, and you'll add them to your map after you explore your goals.

If you're contemplating a PhD, to connect your values to your current activities, it might be easier for you to use the figure on pages 2–3 to first map different areas in your life alongside your PhD. However, if you've started your PhD or are further along your journey, I encourage you to identify three key domains that reflect your activities this semester. For example, three domains for a student in the first semester of a program might look something like this: (1) course work, (2) research subject areas (i.e., comprehensive areas), and (3) teaching skills. A student further along in first year or starting second may, for example, list the following: (1) research proposal, (2) comprehensive exam preparation, (3) conference search and preparation. By asking you to place more than one domain on your map, I'm not promoting the idea that your PhD should take over your life! Prioritize the values you've identified. Make a draft list of domains based on your current activities and where you are in your PhD journey.

Values May Shift in Priority ... Sometimes Often

Values are ongoing and not fixed. You may discover different values at different times during your PhD journey. As you come to understand your values, you may even choose activities and strategies to practise

your values differently every day, or several times a day. How you prioritize your values might even shift from day to day. For example,
when I start my day, after an hour of yoga, I may recognize the value
of compassion in my heart and consciously choose to practise compassion during my student-mentoring sessions for the rest of the day.
Doing this may come easy. But it might be harder to practise compassion if I'm working through a personal disagreement from the day
before. Or, if I slept only five hours the night before, I might need
to start my day with self-kindness so I can show kindness to others.
You manifest your values in your behaviour. Practise your values with
yourself and with others.

If your values are shared – or, at minimum, respected – among the
people you spend the most time with, such as your supervisor, then
you may find it easier to manage minor differences. For example, my
Amma (mother) got very sick while I was writing my doctoral dissertation. The value of achievement declined while the value of caring for
my family and myself increased. At the time, my supervisor's life circumstances differed from mine; however, they respected my values.
I told my supervisor I understood the consequences that my shift in
priorities could have on my writing progress. My supervisor appre-
ciated being kept in the loop. They offered to help me troubleshoot
options. I spent a lot of time writing on trains that year as I travelled
on weekends to care for Amma. Amma reminded me to consider how
this shift in priority would affect me, my relationship with her, and my
relationship with my supervisor. She didn't want me to lose sight of my
goal to finish my PhD. As she recovered, Amma insisted I revisit what
mattered to me. She knew that if "achievement" returned as a priority,
it didn't mean caring for my family no longer mattered. She said, "If
you do not finish, I can't live with the guilt, and you must not live with
the regret." When your values shift, the shift might feel like a simple
ebb and flow; if it doesn't, you'll have hard decisions to make. A shift
in values and priorities might lead you into conflict with your supervisor and supervisory team or personal distress if you don't remain

open to reflecting on your expectations and discussing them with your supervisor. (More on this in Chapter 3.)

How to Clarify Your Values

The ability to identify, set, respect, and reassess boundaries will help you reprioritize your values and, in turn, achieve your goals. Knowing who you are – that is, building self-awareness – is crucial to identifying and clarifying your values so that you can live a values-focused life.

Set and respect boundaries. Boundaries are closely linked to values because, like values, boundaries are linked to behaviours. From the standpoint of refining your values, determining your boundaries can help you think through what you need from yourself. What do you need to practise your values? What do you need from others? Boundaries can also help you manage relationships, mitigate cycles of burnout, and stick to your goals and accomplish them, all of which are crucial during your PhD journey.

Boundaries are the guidelines or limits you establish to represent what you consider reasonable behaviour from others when they interact with you and how you'll behave if others test your boundaries. Boundaries can be physical or emotional and intellectual, and they can be affected by cultural norms and expectations. Physical boundaries reflect a person's sense of privacy and personal space, respect for their body, and gender identity. Emotional and intellectual boundaries can be harder to communicate because they tend to be invisible and are rooted in one's beliefs, choices, and ability to separate one's own feelings from those of others. A key barrier to establishing boundaries is fear of conflict or fear of rejection or abandonment.

Psychologists often refer to setting "healthy" boundaries as opposed to rigid or porous ones. Healthy boundaries enable parties to separate their needs and feelings from those of others, ideally in an environment of respect, in a place where you can agree or disagree with confidence. Setting boundaries requires transparency, clear communication and, when necessary, assertiveness. Here are three steps to set healthy boundaries:

1 Define your boundary (e.g., time, space, what should not be trespassed).
2 Keep the focus on you, not them, by stating what you need (e.g., say "I need Saturday morning to myself" or "I need my Friday afternoons uninterrupted" rather than "I need you to stop bugging me on Saturday mornings and Friday afternoons").
3 Don't overexplain. Keep it simple. State why it's important for you to maintain this boundary (i.e., think about how this boundary will help you meet a goal or have a positive impact on a relationship).

The outcomes of healthy boundary setting include power sharing, having the confidence to share information gradually to build trust, and making decisions without fear of reprimand. In *Boundaries: Where You End and I Begin*, Anne Katherine notes that, like fences, personal boundaries require proper maintenance; there are people who, like ivy, will attempt to creep all over your boundaries. You're not responsible for how others react to your boundaries. If they're upset, they must work that out – it's not your job to do it for them. You might consider saying the following:

Sample: "It's important to me to (or not to) X, so that I can X, which will enable me to X."
Example: "It's important for me to leave here no later than 5 p.m. so that I can attend the weekly exercise class I'm registered for, which gives me the energy to do the work we are trying to accomplish together."

Setting boundaries is not easy for people who are not used to communicating what they want assertively. As Faith G. Harper notes in *Unf*uck Your Boundaries*, learning to communicate your boundaries is a grown-up thing to do. She recommends communicating one's boundaries with "I statements": statements that let a person know how you feel when they behave or do something that tests or crosses your boundaries and end in a declaration of what you want: "I feel X when you X. What I want is X." That's it. That's what it takes to clearly communicate what you need and take responsibility for your own feelings, rather than blaming someone else for them.

If you feel guilty about setting boundaries, please seek out support from people who appreciate that you have the right to set boundaries and who respect you for it. Boundaries also help with goal setting and communicating expectations with your PhD supervisor, other authority figures, and peers. Setting boundaries is foundational to self-care. Boundaries are easier to implement, and stick with, when they're aligned with your values. Having an open discussion about establishing healthy boundaries might feel too intimidating and sensitive to explore with your supervisor, especially when you're just getting to know them. Instead, having a conversation about expectations with your supervisor may feel less awkward for both of you. After all, expectations are often part of the discussion between instructors and students in terms of course learning outcomes. In Chapter 3, I'll suggest broaching the topic of healthy boundaries with your supervisor in a conversation about setting expectations. Later in the book, we will explore how it's also important to respect the boundaries of your supervisor and others you work with, in order to maintain good relationships.

Tell your story. You can clarify your values by exploring stories that illuminate
- a past achievement
- a time when you learned something new
- a time when you overcame a significant challenge.

You might have more than one story that falls under a category. The more stories you can recall and outline in detail, the more you can find out about yourself. The more you find out about what makes you tick, the more you can appreciate what your actions reveal about you. Explore stories that formed who you are and what brought you to this point. You can tease out values, skills, and event chronologies from your life stories.

When you write your story, use the first-person point of view. Use "I" so that your voice comes through. This will feel awkward for those of you used to writing in third person (e.g., "one might consider," "it has been shown that," "they said that"). I shared the origin story of my PhD journey in the Introduction, the story involving youth and bags of shredded purple paper. "The Gift" is a story I wrote in September 2019. Save for a few edits, what follows is an excerpt of the original text I prepared for a digital storytelling workshop by StoryCentre Canada. I took the workshop because I wanted to learn how to create a digital story and explore my values after resigning from my university position:

> When my father, Muriyankulangara Anantanarayan Viswanathan, or Appa, became a citizen of Canada and got his passport, they couldn't fit his whole name on the certificate. So, he went to the notary to get his first name, the name of his village, Muriyankulangara, shortened to "Muri," and his second name, the name of his dad, Anantanarayan, initialized to the letter "A." He kept the name he was given, Viswanathan, so that his name was now Muri A. Viswanathan. It fit on the citizenship certificate and eventually on his Canadian passport. I could always count upon Amma, my mother, to remind us about our roots, so that my sister and I would never forget where we come from, and who we are. Recently – out of the blue – Amma recalled that when Appa changed his name to the shorter version, he felt sad that a part of him was being erased in order for him to become Canadian.
>
> "Viswanathan" is in my name too and derived from Hindu scriptures. It means "Lord of the universe."

Drawing from the work of Nirmal Puwar, feminist Sarah Ahmed has written about women and people of colour as being space invaders when they enter spaces that are not necessarily intended for them. Not having worked outside of the home consistently after having kids, Amma went back out into the paid workforce after my father died, and we lived on the combination of her part-time wages and government assistance. It hurt to see my mother have to work as hard as she did, and to be treated poorly by people because of her accent or skin colour, or because of how she dressed. Like the time she entered the bank manager's office as the head of our household. I remember the look on the bank manager's face when we entered his office. Amma was a space invader too.

My name, my strength; these are ancestral gifts that were given to me. They ground me so that I can choose how to conform and how to resist, and ultimately, how to survive.

I have worked as a university professor. I have achieved more than I have ever expected in academia, and by all accounts I have achieved success. But about a month ago, it became clear to me that surviving within academia was not enough to fit my definition of success, and this led me to choose to quit my job as a tenured professor by the end of this year. I decided to inform the head of my department and to go from there. He said two things when I submitted my resignation. The first was, "I'm really sad that you're going" and then, "I'm confused because no one leaves."

I'm looking forward to the universe of possibilities for work, teaching, learning, and community building ... I feel my world expanding again. I think about my parents and the choices they had to make in order to assert their freedom and to try to secure mine. Because of their sacrifices, I'm now able to choose the future I want and to have the confidence to do so, even in the face of uncertainty. More importantly, I'm giving myself the gift to choose ... I won't give up any part of who I am in order to live the life that I want, and that I deserve.

As you begin to write your stories and collect them, you'll begin to find patterns and appreciate what makes you unique. One reason for writing your stories is to consider all the different scenarios where you shine, especially the ones where you've learned from your mistakes. You get to decide whether you share your stories, with whom, and under what circumstances. Sharing stories can help you find common ground – shared values and shared aspirations – with others. Sharing stories can also make you feel vulnerable, and we'll explore vulnerability in Chapter 6.

Live a values-focused life. Living a values-focused life means living your values in the moment. Your values don't need to be justified, because values are your way of being in the world. Your actions, however, will need to be justified when they impact other people's time and resources. Living a values-focused life means thinking of values in terms of how they pertain to you *and* to others. If you're practising patience, you should be patient with others and yourself.

It might be hard to conceive of your values as being always at your disposal. Choosing to practise or not practise your values may cause you to feel overwhelmed. You might lack resources or the capacity to align your actions with your values. For example, helping others is one of my values, and I *choose* to do things that help me manifest that value (like writing this book!). However, because I'm human and not a robot, I don't always live up to my values when I'm overwhelmed. During times of overwhelm, I'm not always present in body and spirit for others, so I must take care of myself first. I might revisit my boundaries, especially if my values shift, and I might reassert my boundaries to better facilitate self-care. Knowing that I can reactivate my values reminds me that the importance I place on helping others need not disappear forever.

Choosing to practise or not practise your values can be tough, no matter your life circumstances, especially during times when you're in a job or workplace that doesn't align with your values. For example, there were times in my life when I took these kinds of jobs because I needed income and work experience. I told myself I'd "put up with" the workplace until I made enough money and garnered the experience to move on to something better. By "better" I mean a job more aligned with the value of social justice and a workplace where my skills could grow into expertise. (There's the value of achievement again, along with responsibility.) So when I was in a dead-end job, I created a timeline and set a deadline for getting out. I strategized on making connections before I reached my deadline so I could move on to a better job.

At some point in your journey, you may ask yourself, What am I doing here? In the second year of my PhD, soon after I'd finished my comprehensive exams, I went to my first academic conference. Rather than spending the time between sessions networking, I walked around and felt lost. I even stood in a bathroom stall to reduce the stimulation of being around people who I figured were further along their PhD trajectories than me, people who knew what they were doing. I asked myself, What am I even doing here? I thought I must not be cut out for the academic world! Looking back, I was being hard on myself. It might have been a case of anxiety brought on by this "first" experience. I didn't see all I'd done to get there – writing a paper, finding the funding for travel, carving off the time, and so on. Underneath all I'd done to get me to the conference were my values.

As I look back at my much younger self, I could have reflected on my struggles at my first conference and seen them as being part of being an emerging academic. However, at the time, the experience seemed confusing. I could have imagined what my future self would say about the experience in one year's time. Had I done that, I could have asked and answered the following questions and discovered what I value about myself:

• What do you admire about how you handled these circumstances? *Taking time for myself, to gather myself. Perseverance. Courage.*
• What strengths and personal qualities did you demonstrate to get

to that conference and present your paper? *Skills and knowledge.*
*Commitment. Resourcefulness. Optimism. Perseverance. Wanting
to belong and contribute to a community.*
- How did you treat yourself as you were dealing with this struggle?
*Sometimes with kindness, sometimes with judgment. Being too
hard on myself to prove I belonged.*

You might be wondering how I did, after I got out of that bathroom
stall and went into the world again. I'm grateful to an assistant professor who saw my conference presentation. They boosted my spirits
by saying they recognized how hard it was for me to be at my first
conference and that I was doing the best that I could. Then the professor shared their own story: that they were among the first generation in their family to go to university and the only one to earn a PhD.
They showed me that my "firsts" could also be "teachable moments"
in which both the student and the teacher were me.

❋ ❋ ❋

Discovering and practising your values is challenging work and requires
commitment, but it's worth it. You now have a variety of ways to dig
deep and discover your values. I like how Russ Harris, a world-re-
nowned trainer of acceptance commitment therapy (for which values
play a big part), uses the metaphor of the compass to explain values.
Like a compass, don't clutch your values too tightly. Carry your values
in your backpack; take them out when you need to figure out where
you're going. Then return them to your backpack until you need them
again. Values should guide rather than justify actions.

A values-focused mindset fosters flexibility in being true to oneself
through one's actions, including throughout your journey. Identifying
your values involves reflecting upon, and maybe even confronting,
your behaviours through your life stories. There are emotions involved
too. You might not be surprised if some of your values converge with

those you encounter in academia – for example, the value of achievement. However, you might be surprised if some of your values diverge from those of the people you work with, maybe even your supervisor. Values play a role in who you are. How you practise those values inside and outside of your PhD journey will help you arrive at your truest self. Values are about how you want to behave – how you want to live. A deliberate doctorate requires conviction; this will become clearer as you discover your values and plot out your goals in alignment with them.

Map It
After you've explored your values and prioritized them, take your top three to five values listed on page 19 and put them at the centre of the map of your universe of possibilities on pages 2–3. (Other values from your list may rise in priority at another time.) Keep your initial list of domains handy. It will help you explore your goals in the next chapter. Also, keep your list of activities, both inside and outside of your domains. Your activities are how you will practise your values. If you're just starting to contemplate your PhD journey, then your activities might reflect your hobbies and volunteer work. If you're further along in your journey, then I encourage you to further explore the list of activities you've associated with your PhD domains. No matter where you are on your journey, take a moment to reflect on how your activities can help you practise your top values. If you're still having a tough time identifying your values, you may find it easier to derive your values from your goals.

Setting Goals
Aligned with Your Values

2

WITH YOUR VALUES identified and prioritized, you're ready to take the next step – setting your goals based on your intentions (rather than those of your supervisor, your university, or anyone else). Much of the university experience is about goal setting and meeting milestones so that you can move from one year to the next. This chapter gives you permission to lay out your own path, one in which your goals align with your values. Throughout your journey, you'll develop and enhance skills that can be incorporated into your goal setting. Your skills and goals will also determine the activities you choose to practise your values. However, if you're struggling with identifying or prioritizing your values, the exercises will help you derive values from your goals.

What Are Goals?
If values are focused on the here and now, goals are focused on the future. Some of your goals will emerge as you encounter constraints or opportunities for advancement.

In the informal sense, goals can amount to a simple to-do list in one of your domains. In the formal sense, goals require multiple steps to determine how, and whether, you're achieving them. To help you meet your formal goals, you might identify people to whom you'll be accountable. Start by jotting down a list of informal goals in a particular domain. When you have a fixed timeframe for achieving these goals, it might be important to transform them into formal goals.

You can set formal goals by using the SMART system. Each letter in the acronym represents a criterion to outline your goals. Although different words have been used to define SMART, I like how Russ Harris presents the goals in *ACT Made Simple* because they encourage you to link your goals and values to your whole life:

S = Specific, refers to a specific goal that will affect how you act and how you think.

M = Motivated, refers to being motivated by your values and ensuring that your goal is aligned with your values.

A = Adaptive, refers to how the specific goal is going to improve your life. Where will there be impact and how will you know?

R = Realistic, refers to making sure that the scope of your goal is achievable. Consider all the resources, capacities, personal support, knowledge, and skills that are available and accessible to you.

T = Time, refers to putting a timeframe on completing/achieving the goal.

What Are Your Goals?

To identify your goals, identify a domain in a given semester or for a given year. Then write out three informal goals.

For example, I chose "Preparing for my first American Association of Geographers conference" as a domain, and within that domain, three informal goals: (1) write a paper, (2) prepare a conference presentation and slides, and (3) practise the presentation with a friendly audience. For each informal goal, I developed SMART goals linked to my values. When you link your goals to values, keep it simple. Look at your list of values and pick at least one. Here's a breakdown of how I transformed my first informal goal into SMART goals:

⊕ Example
....

Domain: Preparing for my first American Association of
  Geographers conference
Informal Goal 1: Write a paper
Link to values: Achievement | Collaboration

SMART Goals

Specific: Writing the paper will boost my confidence and provide an
  entry into the wider community of my academic discipline. I'll
  think more about how my research fits into community-based
  research practices in North America.

Motivated: Writing the paper links to my values of achievement and
  collaboration. It's my first conference paper and presentation and
  my first collaboration with my fieldwork partners. Building my
  writing skills will help me with future publications and give me a
  sense of achievement and connection with an interested (but possibly uninformed) audience. I want to try writing collaboratively
  with fieldwork and community partners.

Adaptive: Going to a conference with a completed paper will
  improve my life by giving me a sense of accomplishment,
  and it will enhance my academic CV. Plus, I can aspire (i.e.,
  a future goal) to publish a version of the paper or make it
  an important part of my dissertation. I'm eager to write collaboratively (i.e., cocreate, coauthor) with my fieldwork and
  community partners before I delve more deeply into my
  dissertation.

Realistic: Writing a paper is feasible. At the end of my second year,
  I completed my comprehensive exam, and I'm ready to present
  my ideas before doing fieldwork. I have access to financial
  resources (i.e., a university student travel grant) and will have a
  tiny support system at the conference (e.g., fellow students, my
  advisers, and so on). Realistically, I can set aside two hours every

Wednesday afternoon for the next two months. If necessary, I can block off specific times on my calendar to work on the paper. Time: I aim to have the paper done a week before the conference so I can practise it beforehand [Informal Goal 3]. The overall timeframe is three months. I'll approach my supervisor about my intentions for the conference paper, and I'll discuss my ideas with fieldwork/community partners by the end of the term.

....

I develop SMART goals when I'm stuck managing a long-term project and time is of the essence. I also develop SMART goals when I want to stay on track and ensure I'm connecting my values to my informal goals. Note that I link the values to the overall goal first so I can then indicate how the "specific" aspect of the goal is "motivated" by my values. I also maintain a schedule; each week, I look at my completed tasks and rejig my time and tasks as I go.

Many online sources translate SMART as "Specific, Measurable, Achievable, Relevant, and Time." My list of SMART goals is different because they're linked to values. Even though SMART goals are all about "getting that thing done," what I like about having the "M" for "Motivated" and "A" for "Adaptive" is how they keep the doer, you and me, focused on actions and values so that we can align our goals to our actions and values.

By contrast, if we think only in terms of what is measurable and achievable, we can get bogged down in the minutiae of how much of what we do counts and can be measured (e.g., asking whether reading for two hours is productive when the overall goal is writing the chapter). "Realistic," as a formal goal, ensures you focus on a timeframe.

The point is to not let your values get lost in the goal-setting process. Be deliberate. Align your informal goals with your values *before* you create formal SMART goals.

Here's the downside to goals: there's no guarantee you'll achieve them. You can't always act on goals because you may not have the means (i.e., resources, people, or time). It's also impossible to guarantee that you'll achieve your goals, even if you think that you're doing everything that you're told you *should* do to achieve your goals. Sometimes, the best that most of us can do is to seek help to improve our conditions, to ensure we have what we need to keep our goals realistic, and to increase our success at achieving our goals.

Being open to opportunities and constraints is a work in progress, so please don't be afraid to seek out support. You can't know the situations that might arise that could impede or (surprisingly and happily) accelerate your ability to achieve your goals. The PhD journey is a process of change, after all, and it's impossible to predict all outcomes.

Identifying Your Skills

Skills are the means by which you achieve your goals; however, skills attainment (i.e., learning a new skill) and enhancement of your existing skills can also be goals. Consequently, being able to assess and differentiate skills you *have* from skills you *want* is important. You may need a specific skill to achieve a goal. If you lack that skill, then attaining it may become a goal on its own.

For example, say you have a goal to write and present a paper. You realize you need both writing and communication skills. Specifically, you need technical-writing skills and the ability to speak to an audience using persuasion and humour. You are a good writer, but you recognize that you would benefit from studying technical writing and public speaking. Developing your technical-writing and public-speaking skills would become goals that would help you achieve another goal – presenting a paper at a conference.

You come to your PhD with skills obtained through education, hobbies, and other life experiences. Table 1, "The Skills Inventory," is an exercise to help you to determine what skills you have or want to build during your PhD journey.

The inventory includes six common skills categories that you might bring to your program and that you'll likely need during it and beyond.

35

These skills are in no particular order; you're welcome to reorganize them in any order that works for you:

- Verbal, oral, and visual communication
- Written communication
- Interpersonal relationships and self-awareness
- Project management and leadership
- Research and technical
- Other.

You might consider working with your supervisor to highlight skills you need to build or enhance and to identify skills that are not as important.

As a PhD student, you're probably a lifelong learner, so you might think all your skills need to be strengthened. However, I encourage you to identify the skills you feel confident in so you can seek out or create opportunities to practise those skills. Consider your level (i.e., learner, skilled, highly skilled, or highly skilled and experienced) in each category.

- Learner: you don't have the skills (i.e., the ability to demonstrate them).
- Skilled: you can demonstrate exposure and experience in applying the skill to a task.
- Highly skilled: your credentials, coursework, or practical experience showcase your proficiency and confidence.
- Highly skilled and experienced: you can demonstrate a skill and can apply it many times in a particular context or more than one context and in complex situations. You have multiple stories to tell about your knowledge and ability to apply it.

These skills levels are qualitative, and I have done my best to differentiate them. Think of them as a gradual scale from no skill to tons of skills and confidence in applying those skills to multiple situations, and with greater ease.

I recommend working with your supervisor to personalize the "research and technical skills" category for your research area or academic discipline. For example, you might include research methods, computer applications, and innovations that make the most of your knowledge and imagination. Under "Examples of activities," you'll find entries in each category to get you considering how and where you can acquire and practise your skills. Here's your chance to go back to your list of activities to consider additional activities related to skills acquisition and enhancement. Think about opportunities to get training and enhance your skills, such as seminars and conferences. Review Table 1, "The Skills Inventory," and add additional skills categories as needed. Under "Level," do a self-assessment and fill in the circles accordingly:

- Learner ●
- Skilled ● ●
- Highly skilled ● ● ●
- Highly skilled and experienced ● ● ● ●

Jot down activities that will help you gain or enhance skills through practical application.

⊘ The Skills Inventory (Table 1)

Specific skill	Level	Examples of activities
Verbal, oral, and visual communication		
Preparing visual presentations	○ ○ ○ ○	Coursework or internal research seminar
Facility with presentation software (e.g., PowerPoint, Canva)	○ ○ ○ ○	Coursework or experimenting with software on your own time
Communicating your research topic to your peers	○ ○ ○ ○	Course assignments, such as a class presentation
Communicating your research topic to experts in your field	○ ○ ○ ○	University seminar or conference

Specific skill	Level	Examples of activities
Communicating your research topic to a nonspecialist audience	O O O O	
Public speaking (introducing a presenter, talking about general topics)	O O O O	
Presenting an academic paper at a conference	O O O O	
Talking with the media	O O O O	
Giving verbal feedback to a peer about their research or presentation	O O O O	
Receiving and responding to feedback provided by a peer or an expert in your field	O O O O	
Asking questions at a public or research event	O O O O	
Facilitating a group discussion	O O O O	

Other skills: interviewing; lecturing; persuasion; conflict management and resolution; negotiation; describing your feelings; and supervising, guiding, or directing individuals or teams. Consider languages other than your first that you may need for your research or to communicate with multiple audiences. Consider nonverbal forms of communication such as interpreting nonverbal messages, listening attentively, using information graphics, or designing a website.

Written communication		
Communicating your research topic (i.e., generally, with some depth, or with great depth and complexity — you can pick which one is most relevant to you now)	O O O O	Course assignment or internal research seminar
Using technical language in your academic discipline or research area with ease	O O O O	Coursework, independent research, or writing an academic paper
Responding to feedback from peers in written format effectively (and with curiosity and/or appreciation, not simply critique)	O O O O	Coursework or group work

Specific skill	Level	Examples of activities
Responding to feedback from instructors or supervisors in written format effectively (and with curiosity and/ or appreciation, not simply critique)	○○○○	
Understanding protocols for formal email communication	○○○○	
Writing a research grant for funding (specify for yourself or someone else)	○○○○	
Solid command of grammar and spelling	○○○○	
Giving written feedback to a peer about their research or presentation	○○○○	

Other skills: editing, writing for different audiences, writing concisely, numeracy skills, use of different software, creating website content, preparing a teaching plan.

Interpersonal relationships and self-awareness		
Working independently	○○○○	Independent research
Working in teams	○○○○	Group work in a specific course
Self-motivation	○○○○	
Establishing healthy boundaries	○○○○	
Following through with tasks, duties, commitments, or decisions	○○○○	
Knowing when to quit or move on to the next task	○○○○	
Managing diverse personalities on a team	○○○○	
Sharing credit	○○○○	
Expressing your opinions with respect	○○○○	
Expressing your needs, sometimes with assertiveness	○○○○	

Other skills: perseverance, being punctual, the ability to ask for help, setting and meeting deadlines, accepting and acting on criticism, reflection, and cooperation.

Specific skill	Level	Examples of activities
Project management and leadership		
Teaching	O O O O	A teaching assistantship
Helping others to fulfill their goals	O O O O	A teaching assistantship
Delegating responsibilities	O O O O	
Coordinating tasks	O O O O	
Supervising and training peers	O O O O	
Supervising and training learners	O O O O	
Establishing timelines	O O O O	
Strategic goal setting (i.e., short-term and long-term goals)	O O O O	
Time management	O O O O	

Other skills: consulting with stakeholders, technical experts, and other community knowledge keepers; making a project pitch to raise funds or participation; reporting research progress to project participants.

	Research and technical	
	O O O O	
	O O O O	
	O O O O	
	O O O O	
	O O O O	
	O O O O	
	O O O O	
	O O O O	
	Other	
	O O O O	
	O O O O	

This inventory is your first step to identifying which skills you want to learn or enhance. The next step is writing a goal to acquire or enhance a new skill. How will you translate your skills acquisition or skills enhancement into an informal goal and then a SMART goal? What activities will enable you to gain or enhance your skills? Which skills do you want to learn or enhance this semester, or this year? Return to the inventory as you revisit your goals each semester.

Discipline-specific technical skills required for your PhD should be laid out in the admissions requirements. If not, ask about them when you talk to a potential supervisor or coordinator. If you've already embarked on your journey, talk to your supervisor and other students in your discipline who are further along than you. Consider discussing skills development with your supervisor and use the checklist as a starting point for the conversation. Your supervisor may help you determine the skills you'll gain through research, coursework, and professional development opportunities at your university or elsewhere. Your skills inventory is a learning tool – a heuristic device – to feed into your growing self-awareness. As you move along your journey, you can reassess and change your skills list to reflect your changing needs and interests and those skills demanded in your field.

As you gain skills during your PhD and in other areas of your life, you might consider conducting a more wholistic inventory of yourself. Richard Bolles's *What Color Is Your Parachute?* offers an excellent, if not comprehensive, approach to identifying skills linked to the various aspects of your life. Bolles refers to a "self-inventory" rather than a skills inventory. When you have an opportunity to talk to people in your network, industry, and academia, you might ask them what skills they needed to do their jobs or their research and where they obtained those skills (e.g., school, on the job, other professional development). Many job postings in industry don't list the skills required or practised; they list tasks and responsibilities. So you'll need to derive them.

Activities to Connect Your Goals and Skills to Your Values

Have a look at the list of activities you jotted down in your notebook that enable you to practise your top values. Are there activities on your skills inventory that are also on your list of activities? Can you find a link between the activities in your inventory and your top values? As you reflect on your domains, there might be obvious ways to build or enhance certain skills based on the courses available to you. Taking courses might be a crucial activity for you to learn a new skill or improve skills you already have. Try to draw relationships among the different activities you're using to practise your skills. Once again, activities are what link skills and goals to values.

Another way to link skills, goals, and values is to reflect on how a skills category or a specific skill in one category could have wide-ranging effects on several domains. For example, podcasting, a specific skill in the communication category, can enable you to convey information in a format accessible to a wide range of audiences. It is also applicable to research and teaching. Designing a podcast requires you to organize your ideas in ways that are scripted or unscripted. Your design skills will help you engage with the public in formal (i.e., presenting a well-prepared argument or story) and informal (i.e., considering your audience's needs as they emerge through your interactions and improvising) ways. Podcasting, even as a hobby, is an activity that supports your goal of enhancing your communication skills and, perhaps, the value of service and community connection. Verbal and visual communications are broad skill sets that can also be developed as a personal hobby (e.g., visual design, drawing, and podcasting) and applied to different student experiences such as poster design, presentations, and public speaking, just to name a few. How you apply your verbal and visual communication skills can reveal your values. Do you apply these skills to advertise an event that generates income and connection? Does your ability to communicate effectively help you reach audiences outside of academia too? Designing and delivering a podcast may reflect the value of connection or the value of freedom through communication.

Deriving Values from Your Goals and Skills

If you're still struggling to get to the values at the heart of your goals and desire for specific skills, ask yourself these questions:

- What technical or personal skills and qualities would help me achieve this goal?
- What would achieving this goal or skill mean to me or those who witness the achievement?
- What would achieving this goal inspire in others?
- Would achieving this goal or a specific level of skills proficiency cause me to treat others, the world around me, or myself differently?

Introspective reflection might lead you down some dark corridors, but for a systems changer like me, these are questions I frequently ask myself, especially when my values don't align with the institutions in which I work. For example, I value compassion, so when I'm among people who tell me that emotions don't belong in the workplace, I ask myself, Can I spend my eight-to-sometimes-twelve-hour workdays among them? There is the rub. If so, then for how long, and at what cost?

If values are at the heart of your motivations, then they'll shape your goals and the skills you'll attain. Alternatively, you can find the motivations for your goals to determine your values. If you find that the values don't fit you, then you need to ask yourself, Whose motivation and whose values am I working to fulfill? If not your own, ask yourself, Do I really want to be doing the activity associated with that goal, or am I willing to do it to get to where I want (e.g., a higher rank or a better job)? And then ask yourself, How long can I do this and at what cost?

If you're still struggling to link your goals and skills with your values, consider these questions:

- What do I consider most important in my life?
- What personal ambitions drive me?
- In what ways do I want to grow or become stronger?

Set a timer for five minutes and write down your answer to the first question. Don't edit yourself as you write – let your good words roll! Repeat for the next two questions. Once you've finished writing down your answers, read your answers back to yourself aloud:

- What keywords pop out and intrigue you? Are they words that reflect values?
- Did your answers reflect activities you're engaged with? How do these activities reflect your values?

Now write down some informal goals to help you practise those values in different domains of your life (personal and within the PhD realm). You'll need to take some time to transform your informal goals into SMART goals.

✿ ✿ ✿

Being goal-oriented can lead to frustration because once a goal is achieved, the task is over, and you might grapple with the emptiness of "what next"? A goal that is achieved may no longer be relevant (i.e., like marking off completed tasks from a checklist), even though the feeling of accomplishment lingers. However, values can be reflected at any time or periodically as reminders of what matters. What skills do you have and want to enhance? Which skills do you want to build during your journey? What activities will help you practise your values and gain or enhance skills? Is there any overlap among these activities? You can also revisit the skills inventory (Table 1 on pages 37–40) at the start or end of each semester, before your annual reports with your supervisor, or more periodically as part of your practice of recalibration and self-care. As you work through the chapters in the rest of this book, we'll keep coming back to your values, goals, skills, and activities.

Map It

Now that your values are on your map, identify three domains and at least one goal or up to three goals for each. The following figure offers you space to write down one domain and three goals. You'll do this for two more domains.

Domain _____

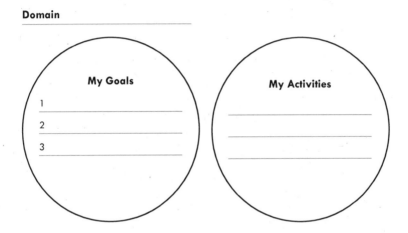

Although I encourage you to link your values more actively to your goals, you don't have to create SMART goals for these domain goals. Simply list your informal goals in the "My Goals" bubble for each domain and look at how your values, at the core of your universe of possibilities, are connected to these goals. Review the skills that you have and that you want to have (or need to learn). Have you listed a skill that you would like to acquire and transformed it into an informal goal? Have you listed a skill that you would like to enhance and transformed it into an informal goal?

Look at all the activities you've listed to this point. Which activities are associated with the goals listed under each domain? In the figure above, write down the activities associated with that domain. Now add this information to the map on pages 2–3. You'll do this again, matching goals to activities, for the other two domains.

Once you have your domains, goals, and activities mapped on your universe of possibilities, look at it. Open your journal and write down the connections that you see. Do you see connections among your goals, activities, and how you practise your values? If you can't see the connections yet, don't worry. Over time, one of your aims will be to ensure that your goals (including skills attainment and enhancement) and your activities are linked to your top values. Remember that as your values shift, your activities may change too.

Making the Most of Your PhD Superuisor

3

YOUR SUPERVISOR IS the most important person on your PhD journey (after you, of course). They are a crucial person when it comes to your research, writing, professional development, and overall advancement through each stage of your journey. Building mutual respect, trust, and understanding are important parts of building a purposeful relationship and establishing healthy boundaries with your supervisor. This chapter encourages you to be deliberate in your conversations with your supervisor, no matter what stage you find yourself at.

Values and Your Supervisor

Before you approach your supervisor to discuss values, you could start a conversation about values with your fellow students in a university career workshop or with students in your department. You could complete an online values assessment and values-clarification survey as a group and discuss the results. You could discuss and explore strategies and activities to practise your values.

Although I recommend discovering your values first so your goals will follow, you might find it challenging to talk to your supervisor about values when you still don't know them well. It's also possible your supervisor has not explored their own values. They may be more used to talking about goals. Consider talking to them about your goals and then tell them how you derived your values from your goals. I hope that, despite the awkwardness, you'll be able to talk about your values with your supervisor in first year, if not in the first semester. You could share this chapter (or the whole book) with them so they can consider how you're developing goals that align with your values to guide you during your PhD.

Questions for Your Supervisor

Before deciding to work with a supervisor, compose a list of questions about their supervisory style, expectations, student load, and research interests. Figure out how many questions you can ask in a thirty-minute meeting and choose the best questions to ask in person. You might be able to ask others in an email before you set up a meeting. You could direct some of the questions to a potential supervisor's current students.

To supplement my own list of questions, I gathered others from sources at Columbia University, the University of British Columbia, and the University of Waterloo and include references in the Further Reading section. Potential questions include:

- What are your expectations in terms of workload, such as the number of hours a student should work per week?
- How would you describe your supervisory approach or style?
- What is your approach to mentoring?
- How do you invest in the leadership of your students?
- What kinds of training and professional development opportunities do you provide?
- Is most of your research collaborative, or are students expected to work independently?
- What kind of support do you offer students in terms of professional development and conferences?
- How often do you meet with your students to discuss their research or progress (as a research team and/or one-to-one)?
- How many students are you working with currently?

- Are you involved in all the stages of a student's research, including publishing?
- What is your preferred form of communication (email, online, or in person)?
- Do you have designated office hours for your PhD students?
- What is your turnaround time when your students request feedback?
- What types of research methods do you consider to be among your strengths? What are the kinds of research methods currently used by your students? For example, do any of them have experience with [insert method]?
- Do you have experiences applying [insert theoretical framework]?
- How do you embed equity, diversity, and inclusion in your research design? In your research practice?
- What policies do you have in place to ensure the inclusion of all your student researchers in your lab?
- How do you integrate new lab members into your team?
- Are the majority of your past students in full-time tenure-track academic jobs? If not, then in what sectors (e.g., industry, government, or another employment sector) do your students work?
- What grants support your lab?
- How many of your students have external funding? From which sources?
- How do you determine authorship on publications?
- Are there any opportunities for collaborations within the lab that could lead to coauthored publications?
- Are there other collaborative opportunities (e.g., departmental, national, international)?

Keep in mind that the graduate studies unit in your university may also have some tip sheets for the kinds of questions that you might ask a potential supervisor.

Setting Mutual Expectations

Setting mutual expectations with your supervisor is another way to explore shared values and establish, if not maintain, healthy emotional and psychological boundaries. Communicating effectively with your supervisor (and supervisory team) is crucial to ensuring that you stay apprised of how their expectations of you jibe with your expectations of them and yourself. A supervisor may not declare how they benefit from working with you – rather, they will more likely focus on what you'll get from working with them. It's important for you to ask a potential supervisor what they'll expect from you and to consider what you'll need from them. Perhaps you had this conversation before you applied for admission. Now that you're in the program, things can change. Check in with your supervisor and begin the discussion of setting mutual expectations.

What Support Can You Expect?

Remember the skills inventory you worked on in Chapter 2? Now would be a suitable time to ask your supervisor about the skills you'll learn and the training you'll receive while working with them. You can reasonably expect to learn some technical skills associated with your discipline, but rather than assuming this, ask them.

If you've been working on building your self-awareness, you might have a good idea about how much assistance you need in establishing deadlines and meeting them. Do you need motivational or project-management support from your supervisor, even initially? If so, ask them for that support and expect that you'll need to build more skills to become an independent and self-sufficient researcher. A PhD is about becoming a content expert, and your supervisor will be more knowledgeable in many areas of your field, so why not determine what you can learn from them?

You might ask how often they expect you to check in with them so that you get a better sense of their management style. Some supervisors ask for progress reports for the entire supervisory committee to maintain open communication among all members.

Your supervisor may have a standard approach to how they work with students; however, each student has unique needs. If you require accommodation for a disability, as is your right, speak to the university's office for persons with disabilities (or equivalent) to discuss processes for accommodation and what you may need from your supervisor and/ or other professors.

Many issues can be addressed if there's open communication between you and your supervisor. Explore how your university facilitates improvements in the equitable treatment of PhD students, including medical leaves, parental leaves, and recognition of religious or cultural holidays. You'll need different kinds of support as different needs emerge during your journey. Don't depend solely on your supervisor to be knowledgeable about these policies.

At a bare minimum, your supervisor will fill out and sign forms and offer intellectual insight into your research. Your supervisor will also play a significant role as a leader among your supervisory team members. Some supervisors are the kind of people who will offer you emotional support and refer you to additional services offered by the university. You can ask your supervisor to provide reference letters for grant applications, scholarships, and jobs after graduation. Ideally, your supervisor will also be a link within the network that you'll build. At times, they will be the central link to your academic network, especially early on.

Being an Asset to Your Supervisor
Because the relationship between student and supervisor involves give and take, consider what makes you an asset on their research team and among their students. In *The Unwritten Rules of PhD Research*, Gordon Rugg and Marian Petre use the phrase "reducing the liability rating" to refer to the process by which a student can come to be seen as an asset rather than a burden by their professor. This may seem harsh, but "being an asset" comes with the understanding that the academic environment is one of overwork. It's vital to use your

51

supervisor's time wisely; in turn, they should do the same for you. Students often jockey with one another for their supervisor's time. You might feel you're competing with your supervisor's other responsibilities and duties when trying to book time with them.

When you have a meeting with your supervisor, consider developing an agenda. As a PhD supervisor, I ask my students to come to meetings with an agenda and to send it to me ahead of time so I can add what I consider to be important items. Our discussions might focus on purely administrative details or something such as a research plan or an upcoming conference. This way, students have some control over the agenda. Other times, when I instigate a meeting, I set up key items and ask students to add their items. Then at the start of the meeting, we prioritize the discussion items together and proceed with the meeting. This approach intentionally fosters respect for each other's time.

When I started as a PhD student, and even when I started as a supervisor, supervisory meetings were often packed with a lot of questions. The meetings went long because our agendas were too packed or because there were too many questions. By the end of our first semester working together, once mutual expectations were established, meetings with my supervisor became more focused. In fact, by sharing the task of setting up and organizing the meetings, we learned about each other's expectations.

What else can you contribute to the supervisor-student relationship? You can bring current information and new ideas to your supervisor. Show them novel resources they might consider. Even though supervisors are experts in their field and know a lot, PhD students often read more and explore avenues their supervisors might not. Take control over the scope of your project and show your supervisor how you're managing things such as scope creep (i.e., how are you keeping the scope of your research project manageable?) so that you can contextualize your research effectively and stay on target to complete your dissertation. (Remember, "R" is for "Realistic" in SMART goals.)

What I've described is characteristic of an apprenticeship, but not all supervisors see their students as apprentices. Nevertheless, to move your research forward, you can do a lot to make the time you spend in supervisory meetings meaningful for you and your supervisor. Keep your supervisor in the communication loop. For example, talk to your supervisor when you're interested in taking on additional volunteer roles or attending or presenting at a conference. They may offer you advice or suggestions and discuss expectations with you. For example, if your volunteer work offers you a new skill that enhances your existing skills or that you can't get through coursework, let your supervisor know. The skill might be important to you, and your supervisor may offer insight into whether the timing of your volunteer opportunity meshes with your research schedule.

If you have an interest in attending or participating in a conference, talk to your supervisor. Your supervisor might expect you to attend certain conferences, and they might have funds to support you as you take advantage of new initiatives. I don't recommend organizing events or panels at conferences early in your journey without first talking to your supervisor. While it's important for you to take initiative, don't leave your supervisor out of the loop. Your supervisor may help you better navigate academic networks (and beyond, depending on their network).

You and your supervisor may become frustrated with each other if you set unreasonable expectations. Take the time to recognize your supervisor's strengths and weaknesses and give them time to get to know you and what you're doing to balance academia with the rest of your life. Remember, you have a supervisory *team*. Hopefully, members of your supervisory team can complement one another's strengths and possibly address weaknesses that your supervisor or other team members might have in terms of knowledge, disposition, or outlook. (We'll look at how to assemble your supervisory team in Chapter 4.)

Don't make assumptions about the flexibility of deadlines or expectations without talking first with your supervisor. For example, neither you nor your supervisor should make a habit of making last-minute requests or not leaving enough time for feedback. Failure to appreciate the limits of each other's time and the depth of each other's responsibilities will whittle away at your relationship. Once again, establishing healthy boundaries will enhance your student-supervisor relationship. Revisit how to set healthy boundaries through the exercises in Chapter 1.

Informal and Formal Check-Ins

Consider how often you want to meet with your supervisor and whether they expect to hold regular meetings (i.e., once a month, every two weeks?). Will your supervisor place the onus on you to ask for and schedule meetings, or will you share the responsibility? Your supervisor may set the stage for developing your supervisory team. Ask your supervisor whether you'll be expected to meet informally or formally with the team, in one-to-one sessions or as a group.

Informal check-ins may include updates on work in progress. They might also be peace-of-mind sessions or professional development check-ins. One-to-one meetings are valuable for both parties, so go in with an idea about what you want to talk about and ask your supervisor what they want to discuss. If you do this, you'll have a working agenda of what you want to get done. Informal check-ins that have only one task (i.e., reviewing a presentation, filling out or signing forms, receiving input on a paper, or checking in "just because") don't require an agenda. Be respectful of each other's time.

In some disciplines, the only time your supervisor and committee meet is at the thesis defence. In others, they may meet during your comprehensive exams, if there are both oral and written portions. Regardless of these formal meetings as a supervisory committee, you might choose to meet separately with each supervisory team member, depending on their content expertise and knowledge. Find out whether your supervisor has office hours for PhD students outside of their conventional office hours, which might be for their courses.

You'll meet with your entire supervisory team to mark formal milestones on the path to candidacy or graduation.

Leaves of Absence

Negotiating expectations with your supervisor can happen at any point, even toward the end of your PhD. For example, early in my PhD, I considered asking my supervisor if they planned to take a sabbatical. If so, would they still communicate with me? If so, how? But I didn't ask. As I approached my dissertation defence, I was caught off guard. I found out my supervisor would be on sabbatical when I thought my dissertation defence would occur. I didn't realize that when a professor goes on sabbatical, they may be, or are permitted to be, out of touch with everyone, even their students. Meanwhile, my supervisor assumed my defence would happen after they returned from the sabbatical (eight months later) and that I'd be able, and willing, to wait.

I was not willing to wait. I was not willing to pay extra fees and defer applying for tenure-track jobs, as academic positions are posted seven to nine months in advance of a position's start date. I could not help but feel that my supervisor didn't think I'd finish before they returned from their research trip abroad. Clearly, our expectations and understandings of each other were not in sync; at some point, there had been a communication breakdown, which led to assumptions on both sides. I felt abandoned when that was not at all what they were doing! They had a right to go on sabbatical.

You can avoid this problem by asking your supervisor, early into your relationship, about their contingency plan should they go on leave. Your department might have protocols in place for situations when supervisors are on any kind of leave (i.e., sabbatical, parental, medical). But they won't always know when they'll be leaving. Sabbaticals require approval and planning, but sometimes those plans fall through or get deferred. Supervisors sometimes move from one university to another or for a different life altogether. For all these reasons, having a contingency plan will ensure that your supervisor's leave doesn't interrupt your journey.

Thankfully, my supervisor and I worked out our differences, but it was a source of anxiety for me leading up to my defence. During my defence, my supervisor was somewhere near the Bay of Bengal, while I sat in Toronto with the rest of my dissertation committee around a boardroom table and a speaker phone. We had to get the university's permission to patch my supervisor in by phone. I was grateful for the collegial relationship among my dissertation committee members, especially with my supervisor.

Relationship Management

Changes and minor conflicts in the supervisory relationship are inevitable and can make managing your student-supervisor relationship challenging. Open communication is the key to managing challenges as they emerge and negotiating your expectations of each other. If your relationship with your supervisor loses its footing, then you may both need to revisit your expectations to try to get back on track. Unfortunately, it might be that you no longer feel as though you're an asset to your supervisor's research team or that your values align. These unfortunate circumstances may lead you to rethink whether you can or want to continue working under their supervision. I hope that you and your supervisor will recognize that conflicts, big or small, are opportunities to build trust.

Addressing your changing needs. I've often been told by fellow supervisors that students become more independent the further along they get in their PhD. As you build your skills as an independent researcher, you may need less research supervision; you might simply need research-progress check-ins and troubleshooting now and then.

However, you may still need to meet with your supervisor about other issues. Depending on the trajectory of your journey, you might face issues that could benefit from the support of, and positive interventions by, your supervisor, including unforeseen personal health events and funding issues. As you venture out into the world of academic conferences, publishing, and the job market, you may need to turn to your supervisor for input and support. You may need accountability when you're writing your dissertation, compared to when you were collecting research for it.

Try not to avoid your supervisor when they're reaching out to you and you feel you're not making the progress you (or they) expect. Academics, professors, and PhD students – by virtue of their environments – can become self-absorbed. As a student, it pays to be clear about what's going on with you and your work rather than leading your supervisor to assume that something is wrong, especially if they haven't heard from you in a while because you've been avoiding them. Avoiding communication with your supervisor does not pay off.

Your supervisor will have lots of competing interests, and while at times it may seem they don't care about you, I encourage you to consider that they do have your best interests at heart. If you're feeling low on your supervisor's priority list, help them see that you believe they have your best interests at heart and be specific when you ask them to share their expertise or time. Start by telling them what you need from them, knowing that your needs will likely change throughout your journey. If your supervisor is not giving you what you need, be deliberate and ask for it.

While the experience of "fading out" or "being ghosted" by a supervisor is not uncommon, your supervisor may not even realize that's what you're experiencing. Yes, it can be scary to state what you need, but do your best and see where the conversation takes you. Seek support elsewhere if the supervisor can't provide what you need. The alternative may be losing your way at a crucial time. If your university has graduate student advocates who can help you manage potential or existing conflicts with your supervisory committee or supervisor, consider adding these skilled peers to your network.

Dealing with absent and intrusive supervisors. While some students further along their journeys might see less and less of their supervisor, others might not see their supervisor much, if at all. Supervisors might not meet with their students regularly; they might send them to a postdoctoral research fellow or research coordinator. I've seen this happen among faculty who are often away on research trips or attending conferences. This is the culture of some large research teams, where student supervision is triaged from one research team member to the next, in order of seniority from lowest to highest. Rather than providing direct supervision, the supervisor signs the student's forms, makes initial recommendations on the research topic, and offers input indirectly. Ask your supervisor about their supervisory practice.

By contrast, some supervisors might intrusively manage a student's research project, preventing them from developing research independence. These supervisors might expect their students to shift their research focus several times to align with their own, which, regrettably, can extend the amount of time a student takes to complete their dissertation. Or a supervisor might pull a student away from their dissertation to devote time to the supervisor's research, still expecting the student to complete their dissertation on time. (This student will probably take more time – longer than typical – to complete their degree.) To avoid working with a supervisor whose expectations and behaviours are not compatible with yours, it's important to talk to them about mutual expectations, but it might be more useful to speak to their other students to learn from their experiences.

In a case of unacceptable behaviour – physical, verbal, or sexual harassment or violence by your supervisor or anyone else you work with – seek help and safety immediately. Find out whether your university has policies in place to address sexual violence and workplace harassment and discrimination and inform yourself of your rights and reporting procedures.

Switching supervisors. If you find yourself with a supervisor who doesn't know how to guide and support you, and if their level of engagement is not facilitating your research or your path toward a PhD, then consider switching supervisors. If you decide to switch, I don't recommend burning bridges. The departure should be as collegial as possible. The graduate studies unit or department may have protocols. It's easier to change supervisors before you've locked into a mutual commitment with your supervisor, but it's not unheard of to switch after your research has begun. You might decide to change your research topic, even if you remain in the same discipline or university department, and you might need to change your supervisor to do your research. Be sure to check with your university to determine whether the process is formalized or informal in your unit

Do you get to fire your academic supervisor? Yes, so long as you have a replacement lined up who will have your back and help you iron out your relationship with the former supervisor, especially when they're in the same department. Paperwork may be required to officially record the change in your department and the graduate studies unit at your university. Before switching supervisors, investigate whether your research funding or any other aspect of your status or ability to complete your degree will be affected, especially if you're further along in your journey. Some research funding is attached to the supervisor, not to the student. Most supervisors will want you to have the best possible outcome. However, try not to be disappointed if things don't go as smoothly as you had hoped. Your soon-to-be-former supervisor may take your decision personally and poorly. If they depended on you to move their research forward, your leaving will be a setback for their research and possibly for your future relationship with them. If this happens, know that you're ultimately responsible for your own success (and happiness) and explain that your decision is professional, not personal. Your relationship might improve as time passes. Try to leave on good terms. But know that sometimes, despite our best intentions, bridges will burn anyway.

I've had two students switch to new supervisors. I try not to think of them leaving me for someone else but rather switching supervisors to pursue their research interests. At first, I was disappointed, but I focused on the fact that it was what the students wanted. One student changed their topic and needed a supervisor with different expertise; they wanted to join a larger research team than mine. The other student wanted to switch to a different degree program at a different department, and they wanted to work with someone else. Both students had scholarship funding that would go with them. Knowing they had funding gave me some solace, but I was still disappointed; they were elsewhere. One of the new supervisors contacted me – I'm glad that they did – and we had a nice conversation via email to make sure there were no hard feelings. I learned from colleagues that they, too, had had students switch supervisors.

The practice of switching supervisors is not uncommon. It requires some foresight and planning, and maybe a few frank discussions with your current and future supervisors, but it can be done.

✿ ✿ ✿

Your supervisor is the most important person (after you) on your journey, but remember that one person can't be "your everything" when it comes to determining the direction of your PhD and your overall wellness. Depending on your supervisor for everything is a dangerous thing – it could lead to their burnout and negatively affect your relationship. However, your supervisor is crucial to the overall sustainability of your research, so learn to set healthy boundaries, including clear expectations. Discussing values early can help build a solid foundation for your relationship. That being said, your supervisory team will also play a significant role in your journey.

Map It

Return to your list of values. Are there links between your prioritized values and your supervisor's? Can you maintain crucial values throughout your activities without jeopardizing your relationship with your supervisor? Now that you know more about your supervisor, your relationship, and whether you have a mutual interest in achieving your goals and practising your values, are there activities you would add? Have you talked to your supervisor about building your skills?

In your journal, write down resources, contacts, funding or conference opportunities, or anything else that can help you enhance your skills, meet your goals, or explore opportunities for collaboration with your supervisor. Add these resources here:

You'll also find a "My Resources" bubble at the bottom right-hand corner of the map of your universe of possibilities (pages 2–3). Add your list from the figure above to your map. You'll add to this list as we delve further into your PhD journey.

Assembling Your Supervisory Team

4

YOUR SUPERVISORY TEAM (or committee, as it was called during my PhD) is the group responsible for guiding you and your research from admission to candidacy to defence. Your supervisory team should be assembled before you submit your research proposal for approval; each university or department has guidelines for when this might be. Your supervisory team is usually responsible for reviewing your proposal and, if approved, granting you candidacy. You can then officially launch your research. Aside from the external reviewer, the people who participate in your proposal or dissertation defence are the same people on your supervisory team. Your supervisor is a key person on your supervisory team.

Building and assembling a supervisory team means bringing together people with diverse expertise to inform your research. They should want the best for you and appreciate your values and goals as they offer guidance. This might seem like a "pie in the sky" notion of what makes for a supervisory team, but it's worth striving for. Recognize your own agency in assembling, and interacting with, your supervisory team. You deserve a supervisory team that can set you on the path to becoming the best version of yourself, as a scholar and researcher.

Values and Your Supervisory Team

Knowing your values and your goals will help you pick your team, in terms of their role and the skills and knowledge they can contribute to your development. Here's the rub: not all of your team members will share your values, but they should respect them and help you achieve your goals.

Consider how they can support you as you live your values in a way that enables you to achieve your goals. If you have people to help you in new and expansive ways, and people who ground you, you can make the most of your skills, interests, values, and goals. Passion is not enough to sustain you. If you have no one to help you figure out how to draw from your passion and live your values effectively (i.e., how to manage the resources, institutional rules, regulations, requirements, and systemic barriers challenging you), then your passion can dry out, leading to unmitigated frustration. A good team, or even one good team member, can help you navigate challenges, provide reality checks, and assess risks. When I've been challenged, having people to talk over my options with was essential. These people were members of my family, my supervisor, a member of my supervisory team, and a planning practitioner, who reminded me where, and if, my research would have relevance.

What Do You Want from Your Supervisory Team?

Your supervisor may be primarily responsible for inviting professors to sit on your supervisory committee. Even if your supervisor picks your supervisory team, or if the university rules say this is the supervisor's role, I'd encourage you to meet with each committee member to introduce yourself, have a conversation, and learn more about them. You don't want to be meeting them for the first time at your first supervisory committee meeting or at your defence. Research potential team members to find out about their current funded research and what they've published. Read their students' dissertations. Observe how they interact with other faculty and fellow graduate students.

When I was doing my PhD, I wanted to talk to potential members of my supervisory team first to see if they'd be a good fit for me. I wanted them to meet me first rather than getting to know me solely through my supervisor or making assumptions about my approach to research. I'd been out of school for ten years, so I was also interested in establishing trust and mitigating any biases the professors may have had about me. In addition to building trust with potential members, I wanted the combination of skills, experience, and perspectives on my supervisory committee to come from a deliberate decision. I told my supervisor I was hoping to make the decision together, after I'd met with potential members. My supervisor was open to that option. However, my supervisor alone chose the external reviewer. In fact, the rules didn't allow me to have a say.

It took me about three points of connection before I could decide whether I could see myself working with someone. Points of connection included taking courses with them, attending their departmental seminars, and reading their books and articles. I then conducted an informational interview – more like a focused conversation. I presented my choices to my supervisor, and my supervisor made some suggestions too. I followed up with one more round of one-to-one conversations. That is how my supervisory committee was established. I wanted my committee members to see value in my work (or at least in its potential), to collaborate with me and, most important of all, to get along, because collaboration and transparency were important to me.

Do They Have Targeted Knowledge and Experience?

Members of your supervisory team should have a keen interest in you and want to work with you to reach your goals, including completing your dissertation. They may remain in your life when you take steps beyond your PhD. They are key people who you'll approach to write reference letters as you apply for grants or scholarships, internships, or jobs. Your team members may offer you different kinds of support, from a shoulder to cry on to content expertise, coaching, or mentorship as you grapple with obstacles and make discoveries.

When you're thinking about who you want and need on your team, consider assigning a value to what they can offer in terms of their skills, resources, and learning opportunities. In Chapter 2, I encouraged you to list skills you have, want, or need to learn. Drawing from your team to learn and practise those skills is acceptable in the learning environment of the university and even beyond your initial coursework. In Table 2, you can chart and rank your wishes for your supervisory team.

📍 Charting Your Wishes (Table 2)

Wish	Not important	Somewhat important	Very important	Who will fulfill this wish? Supervisor, team member, or other?
Someone who is an active listener				
An empathic person				
Someone with experience and awareness of neurodiversity and neurodivergent talent				
Someone with [fill in research methods] to complement my own and those I'll learn through coursework				
A leader in my research area (who may or may not have time for me)				

Wish	Not important	Somewhat important	Very important	Who will fulfill this wish? Supervisor, team member, or other?
A lateral thinker				
A person who has a reputation for publishing with their students				
Someone connected to industry [specify] in my areas of interest				
An interdisciplinary researcher				
Someone with experience and success in activism				
A person with international experience or experience working in my geographic area of interest				
A person who applies the same theoretical framework I use or want to use				
A person with access to networks that could benefit me.				
[Add your own wish]				

Depending on your department's requirements, you might have to include only faculty members from your department on your supervisory team. Or you may be required to include at least one person from outside of your department and discipline. Other programs might allow you to include a nonacademic person who has graduate-level education or is working in industry. You might be able to work with knowledge holders and keepers not affiliated with any mainstream institution, people whose knowledge is derived from their cultural experiences, community status, or activism. Expertise can be found in many places. If a person is not a university-affiliated professor, their participation will likely depend on formal requirements and agreements.

Respecting Boundaries

No single person can be your "everything." You can't expect this of your supervisor. If you depend on one person to be everything to you (e.g., confidante, adviser, and content expert), either you will be sorely disappointed (because no boundaries or expectations were established and followed) or that person will burn out and be of no benefit to you or themselves. Although boundary setting should be a shared exercise, your supervisory team may not instigate the process. Boundaries create and sustain a learning and working environment free from harassment, discrimination, and sexual violence; inform yourself of your university's policies on these matters too.

Respect the boundaries that your supervisor and team members set and those that you set for yourself and declare to others. Without boundaries, you may feel indebted to someone who gives you something you didn't ask for or want, and it's a heavy burden to bear. When parameters are set, mutual respect remains more than a possibility, and indebtedness is replaced by mutual gratitude and learning. I think of boundaries as gifts we give one another to honour and respect relationships; manage our energy and contributions to these relationships; and respect our time, our efforts, and our bodies.

Allies, Mentors, and Sponsors

I encourage you to assign roles – ally, mentor, or sponsor – to signal what your supervisory team members mean to you. These roles will supplement the standardized roles of internal member or external member. Each role reflects attributes that differentiate one role from another; they will help you identify who you need and for what purpose. What are those attributes? You may find them in different people at different times. If you already have a supervisory team, these terms should help you better understand, if not appreciate, your team members. They can help you determine who to add to build a network or complement what your team already offers.

Allies. This is a catchall category. Everyone on your team should support you. Your primary connection with members of your supervisory team will likely be shared affiliation to your university department, or academia in general. But allies can include people who support you regardless of any prior or current affiliation. With allies by your side, you'll be able to better engage with or absorb the impact of any risk you face or undertake. Members of your team should be, at the minimum, allies. Over time, they may become mentors or even sponsors.

In my work on equity and inclusion, the word "ally" is often used as a verb and as a noun. As a verb, "to ally" means building relationships and affinities with one another, ideally based on empathy rather than solely on mutual interest. The term "ally," as a noun, is an honorific that you give to someone else rather than a badge or job title that you give to yourself. You might also have heard of the term "accomplice." Accomplices have the capacity to take on more risks to challenge the status quo. They may use their power and privilege to position themselves beside you. Not all allies are accomplices. If the word "ally" is a difficult one for you, simply use the term "key supporter." An ally will offer you key support on the path to getting your doctorate.

Mentors. Mentors offer indispensable advice and expertise. They can guide you at times when you're unsure about the next steps in your research or in other areas of your PhD. Mentors have content expertise and experience. They share knowledge with you at your request or through experiential learning opportunities that they identify or create with you. Your supervisor may already be a mentor; however, team members may also fulfill this role. They can also show you how to navigate the academic realm.

No single mentor can fulfill all your wants and needs. Aim to have more than one mentor. They can help demystify the environments within which you work, in academia or beyond. If you're a person of colour, you may want to have a mentor who shares your cultural or racial background so that you can learn from their experiences how to navigate the system of whiteness in academia. I had a hard time finding these people within academia. I sought support from a colleague, outside of academia, who I worked with on social planning and advocacy, to help me work through microaggressions so I wouldn't internalize feelings projected upon me or let the microaggressions weaken my boundaries. When I became a tenure-track assistant professor, I found one person, an academic, a few years further into their career, who helped me work through my feelings as I experienced racism in academia. There are now employee groups and subgroups in student associations, not to mention virtual networks, that offer more opportunities to find affinity and connection through mentorship.

Sponsors. Sponsors elevate you and your work. Sponsors either undertake this role formally or step into it informally as situations arise. Typically senior members in your profession or field, sponsors offer insights and invest their time and resources in your potential. They can expect a lot from you, including stellar performance and loyalty, in exchange for guidance, introductions, feedback, and promotion of you, your work, and the work you do with them. A mentor with a passive, nonjudgmental role may move into a more active role.

Sponsorship is not a charitable act; it is a transactional relationship. Sponsors will also gain something from supporting you. I dare say that your supervisor should also be your sponsor because most supervisors possess what it takes to be a sponsor. Most supervisors expect their students to perform and complete tasks, maybe as a member of their research team, in exchange for copublishing works that elevate each other's portfolios. Supervisors can straddle both the mentor and sponsor roles, whether they realize it or not. So the onus may fall on you, the student, to tell your supervisor what you need from them. This is why a discussion about expectations is worthwhile for you, and for them. You can ask your supervisor whether they see themselves as a mentor, a sponsor, or both. I have a hunch that few supervisors are aware that the term "sponsor" can be applied in the academic context.

Sponsors play a significant role in your supervisory team and in your overall network. Sponsors of doctoral students are typically:
- people who are already aware of your strengths and skills
- people who stand to benefit from your work and your research support
- people who have the clout to propel you forward and achieve your goals and who will benefit from doing so.

You and your mentors should reflect on what would be required if they become your sponsor. It's a much more active role, one that will require them to lead and not simply advise.

A Cautionary Note about Power Differentials

I strongly recommend proceeding with caution with any sponsor or sponsorship arrangement, including when a mentor chooses to take on the role without asking you first. It can be difficult to navigate a sponsor-student relationship because of power differentials. For example, if your sponsor ignores your goals and projects their own hopes and expectations on you, they might steer you in a direction you don't want to go, and you might find it hard to object for fear of jeopardizing your standing with the sponsor. Say that, without your consent, they set up an interview with a prestigious professor for a postdoctoral fellowship, but you don't want a postdoctoral fellowship, you want a job in industry. In this situation, you might find it hard to decline your sponsor's offer because you fear damaging your relationship with them. If this sponsor is also your supervisor, you might feel even more jeopardy.

Power differentials rooted in race, gender, class, and ability should be considered in all relationships, including teams with mentors, sponsors, and students. Sponsors, most of whom are from entitled groups, are interested in opening doors for you in ways that benefit them, and this can be disconcerting for those of us from equity-deserving groups who don't come from a long history of entitlement. This is not to say that all sponsors are exploitative. Rather, I'd advise any student to exercise caution and clarify expectations from sponsors every step of the way, just as you would with your supervisor.

While you might want a member of your supervisory team to act as a sponsor, you should not pick a person who is more suited to be a mentor. A mentor guides, so any risk to reputation is yours to absorb. You don't want a sponsor who is only interested in the extremes of power or charity. The power differential between sponsors and students can be huge. A sponsor leverages their reputation to elevate yours. In this type of relationship, the potential risk of predatory behaviour and exploitation faced by a student should not be discounted or ignored. Take the time to know your rights, and if you're uncomfortable with a mentor taking on more of a sponsor role, consider respectfully declining offers packaged as "great opportunities." If you're not satisfied with an opportunity, for whatever reason, trust yourself. There will be more opportunities.

I've always been curious about charitable acts from people I don't know, and I have a hard time processing pity directed toward me. So, if a person invites themselves to be my sponsor, I'm cautious, especially if I can't figure out, or am not given, a solid explanation of what they'll be getting out of the sponsorship. Discourse about sponsorship arrangements often focuses on how they're better than mentorships when it comes to addressing inequities. When I was a PhD student, I was more comfortable with equitable exchanges and reciprocity rather than charity. I despised situations where I was made to feel that I owed something much bigger than what I'd been given.

The closest I came to a sponsorship was when a professor offered an opportunity to take their place at a Commonwealth Women in Planning (CWIP) Network conference in London. They had been invited to give a talk, all expenses paid. I had given a few lectures in their course and loved it; lecturing in their class was a great way for me to get experience teaching on a topic and in a discipline close to my research. The professor benefitted because I presented on a topic they had not been able to address and, in exchange, they provided their input on an academic paper I was writing with the intent to publish. They didn't expect a coauthorship, so they were mentoring me, and the mentorship was something I wanted.

When the professor asked me to replace them at the conference, they suggested I present the paper I was working on. They felt I could make a strong contribution and that it would elevate my exposure globally. I could see the benefit for us both, so I accepted their invitation and went to the conference. This professor gave me the opportunity, and I did the rest. In this example, this person was my mentor and, for the conference, exhibited the attributes of a sponsor.

I'm a bit cautious because I've worked in spaces of entitlement where some individuals with power give a lot less than what they expect in return. You should feel free to discuss what sponsorships in academic environments can look like. Consider opening up a conversation among your student peers about the role of allies, mentors, and sponsors. Involve career counsellors and peer advisers to discuss how allies, mentors, and sponsors can help PhD graduates transition to the academic and nonacademic job markets. Normalizing conversations about power differentials in supervisory committees and mentor-student or sponsor-student relationships will shift the discourse away from entitlements to the subject of support.

External Examiners
When it comes time for your defence, your supervisor will play a key role in choosing an external examiner or reader (a person from outside of your university) for your dissertation committee (an expanded version of your supervisory team). Your external examiner can't be someone you've engaged with formally, such as on a research project, as a research assistant, or even in organizing a panel for a conference. Each university has its own restrictions to minimize, if not altogether avoid, bias (including conflicts of interest) or the reasonable apprehension of bias or conflict of interest. At some universities, the external examiner is not revealed to the student until after the student has submitted their dissertation. Stay in communication with your supervisor, especially if you're considering formal collaborations with people in your field (i.e., more than just networking). You want to avoid bias, real or perceived, and you don't want to enter into a working relationship with someone better suited for the external examiner role.

❊ ❊ ❊

Negotiating terms with your supervisor and supervisory team can take up more time than you might expect. Setting expectations can make it easier for you to turn to them when you need their help to keep your goals aligned with your values. Remember that the roles of ally, mentor, and sponsor can be fluid over the course of your PhD and beyond. I differentiate the ally role from the mentor and sponsor roles because not all allies need to be invested in academia in order to be invested in you. You'll find more allies as you build your network beyond your supervisory team.

Map It

Consider who among your supervisory team can be listed as your people in your universe of possibilities. Using the following figure, list people for one domain.

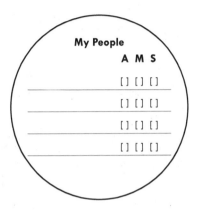

While you might be tempted to list all members of your supervisory team under each domain, focus on what each team member can contribute to your PhD journey and, specifically, their contribution to each domain. Know that their roles may change as your PhD domains change. Indicate whether they are allies (A), mentors (M), or sponsors (S). If you can't determine a person's role but you know their contribution will help you reach your goals in a domain, add them to your list. You can figure out their role later. If you're further along in your PhD, is your supervisor more than an ally, maybe a mentor or sponsor? Do you have at least one person from your supervisory team in a mentor role?

Do this exercise for each domain, and when you're ready, add the names to your universe of possibilities (pages 2–3). You don't have to fill in all the slots. You can leave room for people in your broader network – something we'll explore in the next chapter.

Networking without Feeling Smarmy about It

5

TO ENGAGE IN THE PRACTICE of networking, you need a network to tap into. Ideally, a network will grow with you as your needs change. You are, or will be, the common element that links everyone together. If you're introverted, connecting with people can seem daunting. Even for the extroverted, networking involves reaching out to people who you may know only by reputation, and that might be something new for you. Networks such as academic, industry-based, and professional associations are useful, but the best networks are the ones you build from scratch, because they're individualized and customized for you.

Activating and engaging with your networks is what networking is all about. I like meeting new people, but the thought of networking can make me feel uncomfortable. Introducing myself to people I don't know makes me feel pushy – maybe because I'm an introvert. I feel like I'm forcing people to talk to me while also secretly hoping that they *want* to talk to me. But at its core, networking comes down to having a conversation with someone who you may know because of a mutual interest or with someone that you're curious enough about and want to get to know. At first, your intention should be just to connect with them. After you identify allies, mentors, and sponsors among your supervisory team members, you'll build a larger network, and you'll find more people to learn from and who can support and encourage you.

Building Your Network: The Three Circles

Networks are built contact by contact. Each contact becomes a node in your network that can branch out to new contacts. Building a network from scratch might feel intimidating at first, so try to think of it as a process. Start with a simple task. In your journal or on a piece of paper, draw three concentric circles as in the figure below. Make the inner circle large and the spaces between the rings of the circles large, too, because you will need the space to write down peoples' names.

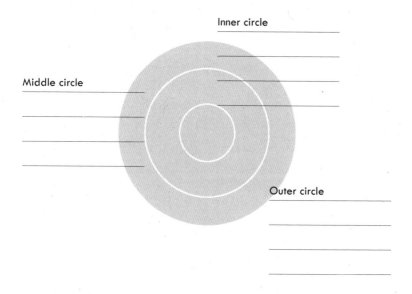

Each circle represents a category of people who will make up part of your network.

Inner circle and primary network. People in your inner circle are part of your primary network. They are the people who know you the best and who care about you the most. These are the people who will tell you the truth when you need to hear it the most. There may be a great deal of reciprocity between you and the people in your inner circle because they're in your comfort zone. Some people in your inner circle will be close friends and family, while others will be in your academic sphere. For example, your supervisor would ideally be part of your inner circle because they're integral to your primary network and a primary source of information and connection with people and resources in the university. Other nonfamily primary contacts may have professional training as wellness counsellors, career counsellors, mentors, or coaches. List the names of people in your inner circle on your diagram. Reflect on what would be the best way for you to reach out to them.

Middle circle and secondary network. If your inner circle is your primary network, then your middle circle is your secondary network. People in your middle circle may be referred by people in your inner circle. They may know you mostly, if not solely, from your academic or other work environments. If your interests straddle both the academy and industry, then the people in your middle circle will include those who are familiar with academia in general, your discipline, or applications of your skills and research. Your middle circle might also include people whose work reflects your career interests. Some may have already seen you work under pressure – in your classes, labs, or the workplace. They may have seen you present your research at a seminar or conference. They may share your values and work ethic or appreciate the same things you do. They might be involved in activities you hope to engage with. Compared to connecting with people in your inner circle, it might take some thought to connect with people in your middle circle.

Outer circle. People in your outer circle may not know you well, or at all. You want to get to know them because they have knowledge or expertise that interests you. To identify potential people, you'll need to do research. Researching someone or their organization is different from creeping them. You need to make sure you have a sense of what they and their organization are about so that you can ask thoughtful questions when you reach out to them. This can be a fun part of figuring out who might be worth getting to know. Most academics' CVs are online. You might start by looking for people who you find to be interesting and want to follow because their work inspires you. Then separate those you might approach from those who you simply want to follow via social media or an online academic network.

Values and Your Network

Learning about the values of the people in your inner circle will likely be easier than in the other circles because you might already know the people and connect with them often. As your goals become clear, you can research people in your middle and outer networks to determine whether you still want to connect with them. Their values may be clear in their commitments, causes, publications, and presentations. Start by considering their activities. Can you derive their values from their activities? Values come through in a person's actions. You'll find out more about them when you meet them. In conversation, you might discover what matters most to them in their work and the reasons behind why they do what they do. You might decide you simply like what their work stands for and want to admire it from a distance.

In Chapter 1, you explored and identified your top five values; in Chapter 2 you reflected on your goals. Maybe you've even developed narratives to align your values and goals, so that you can share your story with people as you connect with them. You may even have a story about what makes your PhD journey an important part of who you are and what you want to achieve in life. These stories can help you to break the ice as you make contacts, thus activating your network.

Activating Your Network

The following steps will help you connect with people in your middle and outer circles. Although somewhat formal, they might help you to feel more prepared, and they might mitigate the awkwardness in building a network of supporters. I'm making a distinction between you building a network of supporters, or allies, and building a network of followers. You can follow people online by clicking a button. Making contacts with people who might inform your PhD journey and support you requires a different strategy. Patience and self-trust are key.

Sending an invitation. When it comes to your inner circle, you might skip researching them and instead invite them to have a conversation. You could ask people in your inner circle to be a source of support, encouragement, and advice. While some might respond with an easy yes, it's always nice to show people in your inner circle that you don't want to take them for granted and why you value them as a source of support.

I recommend doing some preparatory work before you reach out to people you want to include in your middle or outer circle. Email is a reliable platform, but you can also use direct messaging (DM) in social media platforms to connect with people you don't know and for whom you have no other contact information. Sending a DM is an easy way to reach out to someone who is both professionally and geographically located in your outer circle of contacts. But all forms of communication have social etiquettes that change with the times, so you'll need to stay on top of what is or is not acceptable.

I use DM mostly, if not exclusively, for personal messages with people I already know. On the odd occasion I've used DM to reach out to someone I don't know, it's to offer a congratulatory note like, "Congratulations on your new article. Can't wait to read it!" These notes are usually to people in my middle circle, people in my research field or professional network. I like this statement from social media entrepreneur Natalie Zfat, which appeared in Anna Goldfarb's 2019 *New York Times* article "Should You Send That DM? Well…": "DM might not be where you sign the contract, but it could be the place you first shake hands." Another advantage to sending a DM is that you'll know when, or if, your recipient has seen it.

But I still strongly recommend using email to send an invitation to academics. You can say a lot more in a short, well-written email invitation. Email addresses are usually posted on department or professional websites (i.e., research institute, consulting company, or online publication). The first time you reach out to a new contact, you should not ask for anything like a job or a research assistantship. Your aim should be to invite a new contact to have a conversation.

Here are five tips that you can follow when preparing an email to a new contact. You can also apply these tips to a DM, but keep in mind that some of this advice – such as what to include in subject lines – is particular to email.

1 Have a clear subject line that reflects your objective:
   • Second-year PhD student seeking advice and input on trends in [insert academic discipline]
   • PhD student from [insert university or department] interested in learning more about your career trajectory
   • PhD student of [insert name of mutual connection] seeking to connect about industry trends in [their field of work]

While subject lines in email marketing might make or break whether you open an email, when it comes to requests from PhD students, being straightforward is best. Your reader will want you to be honest.

2 Be precise. State why you want to connect. You might open by stating how you know the contact. For example, if your supervisor is a mutual contact and referred you to them, then mention this. Remember that it's easier for people to help you if they know what you want to learn from them. When you reach out, don't make an ambiguous request to "pick their brain." Ask a specific question to highlight common ground (i.e., shared interest in a research area) and increase the chances of buy-in. Common ground will give them a reason to connect with you.

3 Do your research. Show that you've done your research about them. For example, refer to one of their publications or presentations. Or highlight a trend that you're noticing in your field of research about which you're seeking insight.

4 State that you would like to have a conversation with them. I like to say for how long I want to talk to someone. If it's the first time that I'm making a connection, I'll ask for twenty to thirty minutes and add, "or however much time you can offer." Show that you're appreciative of their time.

5 Show gratitude. Close your email with a thank you and a "I look forward to your response" statement. Don't implore or pressure them for a response.

Whether you choose DM or email, you may or may not receive a response right away, or at all. Try to stay positive. If one person you reached out to doesn't get back to you, someone else you contacted will.

In 2006, about a year before my PhD graduation, I sent emails to people in my outer circle. Three weeks later, I hadn't received one reply. Having read so much about bias against South Asian and Asian names on CVs, I thought my last name might have triggered a bias. So, in my next round of emails to new contacts, I slipped in a sentence about how I'd been born in Canada and educated in different cities and universities and how these experiences informed my interests in urban planning. I was troubled doing this (looking back, I still am). I was aware that bias is alive and well, but I felt my confidence dwindle when I received no responses. In another networking experience, a contact heard me talk for the first time and indicated they were surprised by my Canadian accent and elocution. The conversation went downhill from there, even though I gave them a chance to redeem themselves.

Despite these difficulties, someone eventually did get back to me, and then someone after that, and the proverbial ball started rolling. One contact referred me to another, and I became more skilled at figuring out who I wanted to connect with and articulating why. In retrospect, I should have reached out to people to populate my outer circle earlier, probably in second year (i.e., just before or after my proposal was approved and I transitioned into candidacy). Doing so would have increased the number of my allies and potential mentors. I would have been more practised at networking. That being said, it's never too late to start building your network.

Preparing for a focused conversation. After a contact has accepted your invitation and you've done your happy dance, it's time to prepare for your conversation. Remember, the purpose of the conversation is to connect. How will you focus the conversation? Look at the notes from your research and the subject line in the email you sent them. Pick one primary topic to ground your conversation. Identifying a secondary topic can be good for follow-up questions, if there's time, or for future conversations.

Focused conversations can provide you with career-enhancing information (e.g., questions about life in academia or details about an industry that might fit with your skills or doctoral research). A bit of awkwardness is normal if you don't have a lot of practice doing interviews. But don't be afraid to go with the flow. Preparing questions ahead of time can make the conversation feel a bit less intimidating and can impress your contact by making the best use of the time you have together. Have enough questions for a twenty-to-thirty-minute conversation; you can modify the number of questions you ask based on the amount of time available.

Open with a general question as an icebreaker:
- Can you tell me a bit more about your journey to [insert where they are now or their current position]?
- As a PhD student, I'm curious about how you went from your PhD in [name discipline] to what looks like a fascinating career in [name of industry or university]. Can you share a bit about that path?

- Did you always know you wanted to do a PhD?
- Did you always know you would go into industry after your PhD?
- Can you tell me about how you transitioned from your PhD to your postdoc to your role as a professor?

"Yes/no" questions will lead to shorter answers than open-ended "how" or "tell me about" questions. If you have a background in qualitative research, this is good time to draw from your experience in designing and/or conducting interviews.

After your opening question, move on to a content-oriented question about their job, their research, or a recent paper or a presentation you witnessed, depending on your primary focus. You might ask them for insights into trends in your field or in their specialization. Try to include two questions – one about what their goals were during their PhD and one about what their goals were after completing their PhD. Their answers may offer some insight into the purpose of their doctoral journey. Doing so would also reveal their values.

As in your invitation, show gratitude for your contact's time, during the conversation and at the end. Although you shouldn't ask for anything, you can ask for a referral to another contact in their network. It's fair game to ask a question such as, "Based on what we talked about, is there anyone else who you think I could benefit from talking to?" Follow up with your contact right after the conversation with an email to say thank you. Make it brief and courteous. Showing gratitude leaves a good impression.

I encourage you to test your questions with peers, your supervisor, and supervisory team members, or others from your inner circle. Find out how your questions land with them (i.e., Do they feel it's too much like an interview or, worse, an interrogation?). Ask them for tips to stay calm and focused when making new contacts. Check in with your own comfort level after practising your questions and conversation topics.

Don't feel pressured to hold a conversation or informational interview by videoconference if you don't want to. Having a conversation over the phone works too. Do what feels the best for you. Power differentials, the human condition of unconscious bias, and gendered dynamics affect our experiences in meeting people, especially for the first time, and they feed into the dynamic of online networking and being seen on screen.

Informational interviews, especially if you're interested in planning your career after your PhD, although more formal than having a conversation, are useful too. Prepare your questions and focus on career planning. Again, don't make requests of people you're just meeting for the first time. Your aim is to connect.

Feeding Your Network

Once you've talked with your contact and sent them a short thank-you note by email, reflect on what you've learned. How did you feel about the conversation? Do you want to remain in touch with the person? Would you consider asking them for advice in the future? Did they offer to stay in contact? Do you think you'll want to follow their work or share your work with them? Now that you've made contact, you can feed your network with an update via DM, social media, or email? (Jump ahead if you want to read a bit more about social media and online networking, but come back afterwards!) Contact those with whom you felt the most connection.

Times to reconnect and provide an update can include:

- before a conference where you know your contact is presenting
- before your own presentation or participation in a webinar to inform them that you'll be attending or invite them to attend
- when you publish something or receive accolades, especially if you cited your contact's work
- after you've reached a milestone (i.e., did a conversation from your focused conversation help you reach a milestone and you want to show gratitude?)

Social Media and Online Networking

Search for social media platforms by key terms such as "academic" or "PhD" and many options will come up. While it would be hard to contest that social media plays a big role in keeping people connected, it can take a lot of work to build and curate a social network. Take your time identifying and following academic authors and researchers. Find people whose ideas and work you admire, and identify publications that you, your supervisor, and other people you work with consider relevant in your field. Some social media platforms, and even traditional websites, will cater to the needs of PhD students, addressing diverse topics such as applying to specific scholarships, how to create infographics, approaches to publishing and editing scholarly articles, research ethics, dealing with peer review, and analyzing statistics. Social media is crucial for monitoring trends in research and industry and seeing who's sharing whose work in the wider universe.

Are you a consumer or producer of information or both? As a consumer of social media, you may passively consume information, news, and perspectives. Or you could be much more active in your consumption, taking and applying the information that you receive. You're a researcher, so be discerning when you consume information on social media and when you share it. Sharing information automatically turns you into a producer. You can engage in social media by simply learning from information. You can determine how much control you want or need and how visible you want to be – all things you're likely familiar with from nonacademic social media platforms.

If you choose to be a producer of information and add statements to what you're reposting or sharing, take time to craft what you say and how you say it. Some statements breed reactionary quips rather than considered responses. Write your post in a document first and have a third party review it before you post it. You'll have an opportunity to check if what you're saying can be misinterpreted or whether someone may take offence.

Consider whether you'd like to share information in long form, such as a blogpost or extended online article, to explore multiple facets of a topic or issue more fully than you could in a post. Or are you more comfortable writing and sharing your thoughts in a short message? Most people on social media are unskilled archivists, people who are searching for and storing information and sometimes eager to share but not likely to research and check the validity of information.

There are places to network online outside of social media. As my PhD students remind me, online cafés exist where students can share their experiences, successes, and struggles with article submissions, competitive grant or scholarship applications, and job interviews.

Choose how you want to engage with social media and online platforms. There are risks involved. Research platforms before you join them. Take the time to observe activity on the platform before you engage. Review guides about the use of privacy settings. While most items posted on social media are there forever, you can investigate options for time-limited content – often through "stories" or other applications and functions – which might be more appealing to you. Be deliberate about how you use technology to connect, communicate, and build relationships. Technology speeds up communication, but the social practices surrounding technology use can change rapidly. A direct message feels like a private message, but it can be shared (the "social" aspect of social media).

I'm far from being or becoming a social media maven, so I've provided additional resources in the Further Reading section. These sources address the etiquette of social media, such as direct messaging a potential contact, taking a stand on a topic, and dealing with negative reactions to social media posts.

Building a Community of Practice

Conducting research and writing your dissertation can feel isolating. To beat the isolation, consider creating a community of practice (CoP) – a small-scale in-person or virtual network. A CoP is a group of people who share a common interest, concern, or desire to learn and exchange ideas on a regular basis.

The term "community of practice" was coined by Etienne C. Wenger with Beverly Wenger-Trayner and William M. Snyder, who identified three key elements to a successful CoP: (1) a domain, (2) a community, and (3) a practice. "Domain" refers to a group's shared common ground. The domain is a foundation for building trust, knowledge, and appreciation – a way to build bonds, share successes, and learn from mistakes. "Practice" is literally practising what is learned. Think of the CoP as a group with whom you can test ideas, share works in progress, and experience gentle accountability.

A research-oriented CoP can include those in your academic discipline or engaged in your research topic, or simply researchers from your cohort (i.e., researchers in the same year of study). Indeed, the possibilities are endless. Holding meetings online means you can involve researchers outside of your university and geographic region and facilitate participation by a wider network of people.

Don't Forget Your Friends!
Your friends may be people in your cohort who you've bonded with during your PhD journey. They could become contacts who will help you branch out and expand your network, especially after you graduate. You'll have friends who fall into your inner circle or middle circle. These are people who will empathize with the stress and workload you're undertaking, in a way that those outside of your program may not be able to appreciate. After all, they're on their own PhD journeys. Working with your graduate student association or career centre, you could establish a broader interdisciplinary peer network to foster camaraderie. A broader network of graduate students can ease transitions at all stages of your PhD journey.

※ ※ ※

Networking involves give and take. Remember, there's fluidity across the inner, middle, and outer circles of your network. A person from your outer circle might migrate to your middle or inner circle as you build your relationship. Your network members' values and goals will surface as you get to know them, read their writing, and have conversations. How they react to your interests and priorities will also give you a sense of who they are and what makes them excited! The three circles of contacts in your network will become your people.

Knowing how to request a focused conversation or conduct an informational interview will become useful as you assemble research teams, committees, and conference panels in the future and as you get closer to exploring your career options inside or outside academia. I've used this approach to networking several times in my life: during my PhD (as already noted, I should have started earlier), as a new professor, and even when I was planning my academic sabbatical. Networking played a big role in my successful departure from academia and success as a solopreneur. With a network, you'll never have to undertake your PhD journey, or any career path, completely alone.

Sometimes you can get stuck in thought patterns that become obstacles to success. That's why you should have people in your inner and middle circles who can call you out on your shortcomings and biases, people who know when you're getting stuck. Would you call them an ally? Are you the kind of person who has a hard time asking for help or recognizing when you need help? If so, consider having a person from your inner circle to help you when you're unable to help yourself.

Map It

Who are the people in your inner and middle circles from whom you feel confident about seeking support? Put their names in the appropriate circles in the following figure. In the outer circle, put the names of people whose work and experiences have you curious and interested and whom you can see becoming people in your inner and middle circles. Writing down the names of potential or existing contacts is a tangible, realistic starting point for identifying your people, including people outside your supervisory team. If you have more names than you have space for in the figure, then keep a key list in your journal and draw from it in the future. When you're ready, transfer the names from here to your universe of possibilities (pages 2–3).

My Network

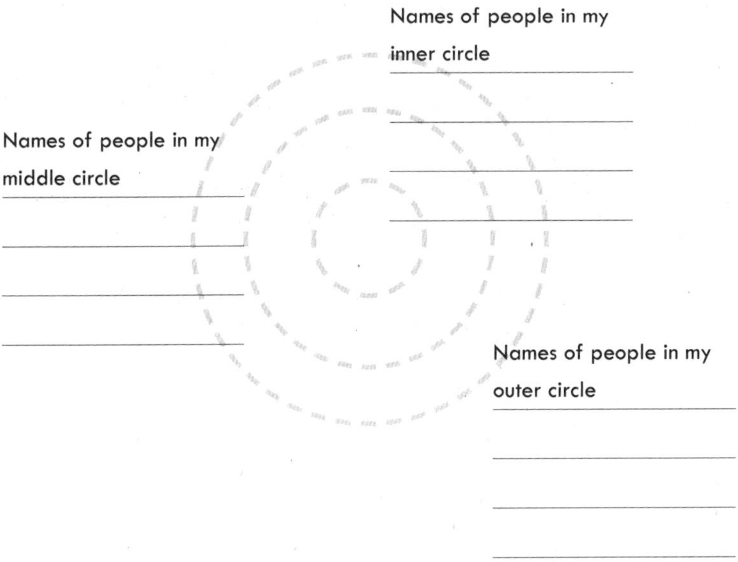

Names of people in my
inner circle
_____

_____

Names of people in my
middle circle
_____   _____

_____

_____

Names of people in my
outer circle
_____

_____

_____

Take a look at your universe of possibilities. Are any of the people in your inner and middle circles "My People" who can be listed under a domain? Can any of them be allies, mentors, or sponsors? If yes, then give them that designation. If not, then list them without further designation. Your map is your work in progress. You can add information as you gain knowledge about yourself and your network. Keep in mind that, over time, your allies may become your mentors or sponsors.

"Feeling All the Feels" through Your PhD

6

YOU'LL EXPERIENCE A WIDE spectrum of emotions (your own and of other people's) throughout your PhD journey. As a student, and simply as a person, you'll experience more than one emotion at a time. But the mix of emotions felt by PhD students combined with power dynamics and competing expectations in academia make for a particularly complex cocktail. Emotions should be accepted as a normal part of the PhD journey. Learning to express what you feel and understanding your own vulnerability are crucial to managing relationships, resolving inner conflict, and maintaining wellness.

Experiencing loneliness but hiding your emotions often translates into private suffering and heartbreak. It doesn't have to be that way. As this chapter shows, being transparent about your emotions will help you see how your values and goals (and the people in your network) can contribute to your mental well-being. Keep in mind that the sections in this chapter only scratch the surface. I've provided resources in the Further Reading section so you can dig deeper. Seek guidance and support as you work through your emotions.

Naming, Expressing, and Receiving Emotions
In any given situation, you might find it challenging to name the emotions you're feeling. You might have been encouraged not

to tell people what you're feeling because, in academia, what we think often trumps what we feel. In *Nonviolent Communication: A Language of Life,* Marshall B. Rosenberg argues that not expressing our feelings has a heavy cost on our health and our relationships. Rosenberg advocates for an approach called nonviolent communication, or NVC. In it, how you feel (e.g., disappointed, impatient, frustrated) is differentiated from how you think you are (i.e., inadequate). Rosenberg provides a list of almost 150 feelings so we can build our own vocabulary of feelings to reflect "how we are likely to feel when our needs are being met" (e.g., adventurous, happy, spellbound) and "how we are likely to feel when our needs are not being met" (e.g., aggravated, fearful, overwhelmed). Rosenberg notes that we don't even have to use the word "feeling" when we express our emotions.

There are many resources to help you name your emotions. In Gloria Willcox's "The Feeling Wheel," names for feelings fill out the inner and outer spokes. The wheel differentiates primary feelings from secondary feelings. Willcox's work has been used by many organizations, including the Canadian Mental Health Association, to build awareness of the different human emotions. The Further Reading section will lead you to more resources.

My early career as a community planner taught me a lot about how to communicate with different groups and how power differentials affect not only the ways we communicate but also how experienced people express their feelings in a given space. While I take pride in my emotional intelligence, I've learned that it's not possible to know exactly what another person is feeling at any given moment without asking them, and this is, in part, because their behaviours match what we think they're feeling. For example, you might see tears dripping down your friend's face. You might think they're grieving. But if you ask, you might learn they're overjoyed about getting a job. A new job, they tell you, means a new start, which is both exciting and scary, since moving away means making new friends and venturing farther away from family. They might not know the words to tell you exactly how they're feeling, so simply connect to what they're feeling.

To put yourself in a position to receive other people's feelings rather than becoming enmeshed in them, consider the following:

- Don't make assumptions about what a person is feeling or how they're expressing their feelings.
- Be aware of boundaries (of "where you end and they begin," as noted by Anne Katherine, Brené Brown, and others) so that you can show your empathy or compassion.
- Showing empathy means respecting other people's autonomy. Their feelings are associated with their experience(s), not yours. As Brown advises in *Atlas of the Heart*, try to connect rather than relate to what a person is feeling about their experience.
- Try to connect to what a person is feeling without judging them.

Learning how to name our emotions is crucial if we want to understand them; however, many adults never learn how to do this. Too often, the fast pace of academic environments leaves little time to identify what and how you're feeling at a given moment. Take the time to learn how to express what you feel, and encourage your peers to do the same. But respect one another's autonomy.

Stress and Vulnerability

Consider ways to recognize feelings of stress, the situations that incite them, and how to heal so that you can move *through* your emotions. Hans Selye's research has influenced how society uses the term "stress" to describe the factors that cause our bodies to react to different conditions, outside of those that might make us want to fight or take flight. Prolonged stress can influence conditions such as heart disease. According to renowned trauma and addiction expert Gabor Maté, when you supress your emotions, you suppress your immune system. When there's a constant and persistent feeling of stress in our learning environments, and when these conditions become normalized (i.e., the cult of being busy), it can affect our ability to learn (and teach) and take risks. Stress can erode trust and increase feelings of vulnerability.

Research on vulnerability, as presented by Tarana Burke and Brené Brown in their edited volume *You Are Your Best Thing: Vulnerability, Shame Resilience, and the Black Experience,* reveals that not everyone bears the same risk when they share their emotions. Showing vulnerability involves social and emotional risks, and these risks are influenced by our experiences and identities. Differences in power and status are factors that increase the vulnerability of members of equity-deserving groups who are living within systems dominated by whiteness and by the normalization of heteronormativity and ableism. In turn, there's a politics of vulnerability that feeds stress.

The pressure to achieve academic excellence fuels stress among students and faculty in university environments. Until universities change work and learning spaces to make it easier to manage, if not minimize, stress, it will be difficult for you to overcome stress. Doing nothing is not an option, at least not without a cost to your physical health and mental wellness. So it makes sense to me that many students and faculty, especially people from equity-deserving groups with histories of societal exclusion and erasure, are averse to what Shawn A. Ginwright calls "social and emotional risk-taking" outside of spaces where safety and mutual support are cultivated.

Not everyone experiences the same risks in showing their vulnerability. I became more willing to share stories about my own vulnerability when I became more secure as a tenured faculty member. As an untenured professor (with less job security) and as a graduate student (with less power), I felt less secure. As a tenured professor, I no longer considered my vulnerability a weakness; however, I remained cautious about expressing my vulnerability in general. I was aware that many of my peers, and even some of my students, perceived vulnerability as a weakness. As a cis and able-bodied woman of colour, I was uncertain about what I needed to do to set the best example for my students. Because of my experiences working with South Asian youth, who were integral to my decision to pursue a PhD, I felt especially accountable to students of colour.

Looking back, I recognize that, in university spaces, expectations for me were often out of sync with what I really wanted, and many times my capabilities were underestimated. I'm not unique in this sense. My experience of applying whatever agency I had at times felt like a game of hopscotch where I marked a point along my path, hopped forward to remove a barrier, and then sometimes, arms akimbo or wobbling on one leg, I'd forge or wobble ahead to my desired finish line. Even now, I decide who deserves to receive my stories, and I choose how and when to share them.

During your doctoral journey, you, too, will have to learn how to manage stress, explore what it means to be vulnerable, and acknowledge the risks you may face in speaking out. All too often, the onus is on the individual to practise self-care. I encourage you to engage in conversations with your peers about university workplace inclusion and mental wellness, about scheduling breaks in your work timetable to do nothing, about the importance of preserving personal time and balancing work with the rest of your life. These conversations are crucial to normalizing wellness as a societal or institutional task rather than an individual one.

Reaffirming Your Values and Boundaries

Reaffirming boundaries can help you manage stress and interpersonal conflict and facilitate emotional expression; doing so also reaffirms your values. As noted in Chapter 1, boundaries offer ground rules for you to determine what is and is not acceptable so you can ensure your own emotional, physical, and psychological health and safety. Boundaries are an essential part of self-care. When stress becomes overwhelming, it's a good time to check in with yourself, to consider whether your boundaries have become permeable or imbalanced. Is it time to "fix the fence"? While it may not be possible for you to extricate yourself entirely from the path of someone who doesn't respect your boundaries, consider ways to minimize interactions or seek assistance from a third party to help manage your boundaries and re-establish them in your relationships. Be patient, go slow, and use means of expressing your feelings (e.g., your voice, your writing, power channels) to advocate for yourself. Practise the "I" statement in Chapter 1 to communicate healthy boundaries, recalibrate, and find balance.

Rethinking Imposter Syndrome

The term "imposter syndrome," coined by clinical psychologists Pauline Clance and Suzanne Imes in 1978, pathologizes the recurrence of anxiousness among high achievers and rationalizes stress as part of a high-performance academic culture. The term describes the persistent self-doubt experienced by intelligent, talented, high-achieving women that leads them to not own, or believe in, their success. The high-achieving women in the study believed they'd "fooled" people into believing they were intelligent and capable. Pretty much anyone, including PhD students along the gender spectrum, can experience imposter syndrome if they're grappling with intense self-doubt and credit others or luck for their success.

I dislike how "imposter syndrome" pathologizes self-doubt. For most folks, self-doubt is part of the creative and problem-solving processes. Anyone learning something, or experiencing a situation for the very first time, will experience self-doubt. I especially dislike the term because conversations about imposter syndrome focus on the individual rather than on systemic issues that feed self-doubt, lack of confidence and, eventually, distress. If an individual's struggles with perfection, overcommitment to work, childhood expectations of genius and expertise, and even experiences with socialization can affect their self-confidence, so too can systemic biases and exclusions.

Racialized people and people from other equity-deserving groups are often treated as imposters in academia, regardless of how confident, intelligent, and talented they are. As a cis woman of colour, the daily experience of contending with and defending myself against microaggressions in the workplace could wear me down and suck out the juicy energy that I've worked so hard to build and sustain; this is on top of the pressure to excel in academia. I'm often surprised by the amount of work, not to mention the emotional and financial expense, it took to sustain energy in my academic life to make room for joy in achieving my dreams.

As a student, you may struggle to overcome your feelings of fear and self-doubt associated with imposter syndrome. Seek help to work through these feelings. Confidence is rooted in socialization, and showing empathy for yourself and others is a skill to develop. Given the ongoing need to build inclusive practices in education (e.g., in the classroom, curriculums, research, and policy), I encourage you to collaborate with your fellow students and people in your inner circle to normalize feelings of self-doubt and burn the term "imposter syndrome." When failure is discouraged and frowned upon, and when few examples of academic risk taking are shared or modelled, then student flourishing is stunted. If we had collective support to work through self-doubt, and if there was no expectation that we, as individuals, must "fix" everything ourselves, then we'd all occupy spaces where self-doubt and learning how to be a learner (i.e., "not there yet") are accepted. We'd have a collective source for active introspection and practising self-awareness in academia. Consider talking to your supervisor or mentors about ways you can overcome feelings of self-doubt. Consider asking your supervisory team members about times when they may have experienced self-doubt and how they coped with these experiences. My hope is that holding these discussions with people in your inner circle will show you that you're not alone in working through feelings of self-doubt.

Combatting Burnout and Empathic Strain

Feeling ineffective is a symptom of burnout, and sometimes it can feel like a never-ending battle. The World Health Organization defines burnout as all-encompassing (i.e., physical, mental, and emotional) feelings of exhaustion and distance from one's job (i.e., depersonalization), including feelings of cynicism that impact a person's ability to do their job. Burnout is related to workplace conditions. Burnout can be addressed if we take a break from doing the work or, more importantly, change workplace conditions to facilitate long-term engagement and efficacy on the job. In *Can't Even*, Anne Helen Petersen refers to burnout in millennials as tantamount to living with a never-ending to-do list and attempting to fulfill, often unsuccessfully, one's passions through work. The cyclical aspects of burnout, as a workplace condition, are experienced across generations and sectors.

Burnout is common among PhD students. Factors that can contribute to it may include

- stress
- lack of motivation
- declining trust in one's supervisor or academic colleagues
- a reduction in the quality or speed of communications with your supervisor or other researchers
- feeling that your employer doesn't compensate you for doing your work
- not feeling heard or having your voice amplified
- lack of vacation days or time off
- twenty-four-seven work culture
- feeling like you're always playing catch-up.

When emotions are not expressed, they build up, leading to emotional exhaustion, which translates into more stress. Burnout can reoccur in a cycle. Building ways to recognize, express, and validate emotions will lead to more supportive PhD communities.

Burnout also has systemic roots. While it might make sense to talk to your supervisor about the culture of overwork, I appreciate that this is easier said than done when power differentials are in play. Addressing recurrent cycles of burnout at the individual level requires changes at the systems level too. Rich and sustaining relationships, equitable pay, self-care, and professional development can help change work conditions. At the individual level, focus on the pillars of health: good nutrition, enough sleep (learn what "enough" means for you), and exercise. Finding connections with others – friends and loved ones – can also be part of self-care. Having people to talk to, hang out with, or do nothing with can provide a sense of belonging.

Burnout cycles are associated with other stressors – situational or long-standing (i.e., chronic) – that put a person at risk of empathic strain. Empathic strain, also referred to as compassion fatigue, is more than burnout. According to Françoise Mathieu, empathic strain or compassion fatigue "is characterized by profound emotional, mental, and physical exhaustion" (all symptoms of burnout too) developed during one's experience or career of offering care to clients, peers, or family members. It can translate not only into a lack of empathy for others but also into a lack of empathy for oneself. Empathic strain goes beyond one's feelings of overwhelm on the job and deepens one's feelings of disillusionment about the world overall. People who have been at their job for an exceptionally long time can experience empathic strain because it's linked to feelings of helplessness and loss of hope that anything will change.

PhD students who juggle a few jobs with their studies to make ends meet and who have family caregiving responsibilities, or who are trying to bridge cultural expectations and community commitments, are also at risk of empathic strain. If this is your experience, then professional help may be necessary. Connecting to your inner, middle, and outer networks for input and assistance is highly recommended. Remember, working through something (rather than getting over something) might take longer, especially when there's healing to be done and systems are slow to change, but the benefits to your well-being will last longer.

Common Reasons for Leaving a PhD Program

According to a 2019 PhD Survey conducted by *Nature* magazine, the top reason students leave or drop out is lack of funding. The second reason is the extended length of time it's taking to complete the degree, sometimes beyond the limits of university regulations.

Funding and time to degree (TTD) are closely related. If you don't have consistent, adequate funding to pay for tuition, living expenses, and your research, then you'll have to work, and you'll likely take more time to complete your degree. "Funding" refers to money provided by an organization, university, or government. It can take the form of a scholarship, teaching assistantship, or research assistantship. Sometimes, you'll get money in exchange for work, as in the case of a teaching and research assistantship; other times, you'll get money without expectation for work, as in the case of a scholarship. Look into your university's labour and employment rules and, if relevant, collective agreements for assistants. If you need to seek employment beyond an assistantship to make ends meet, there may be employment rules to consider.

"Financing" refers to borrowing money with an expectation that you'll repay it, often with interest, within a specified time (e.g., a loan or line of credit). A lot of focus is put on funding graduate degrees rather than financing them. But even if you receive funding for your PhD degree, it can run out, not necessarily because of a lack of financial management but because funding to a program or professor may end. Some grants have TTD regulations (e.g., funding will stop after a student has reached the fourth year of a four-year degree). If you need an extra semester to complete your dissertation, talk to your supervisor and find out if your funding will stop. Find out if your university will offer "bridge funding" to help you to finish your degree.

Sometimes poor communication and incompatible expectations between students and supervisors can force students to extend the TTD. (See Chapter 3 for unacceptable behaviours by supervisors that can affect TTD.) Extending TTD puts pressure on finances, which breeds stress and can weaken mental wellness. It's a vicious cycle. If this happens to you, seek out support from your inner, middle, and outer circles – all of them – to troubleshoot problems with financing; it's even more important to manage feelings of internalized guilt and shame. Guilt, shame, and disappointment are associated with not meeting expectations – a program's, supervisor's, or peer group's expectations. These feelings of guilt and shame are all too common among PhD students who choose to leave, willingly or unwillingly.

Fighting the Sunk Costs Fallacy

What about if you decide to stay in a PhD program against your better judgment? Maybe you've decided you've already sunk (i.e., invested) so much time, money, and more into the endeavour, it would be a waste of money to pull out. This phenomenon is referred to as the sunk cost fallacy because the reasoning is unsound: you want to leave, and you can leave, but you don't leave. You may be afraid of making the wrong decision or losing something, or maybe you're simply avoiding making a decision.

The key is knowing what you want within the context of what is possible. Aligning your activities and goals with your values can help you remain focused and attuned to your feelings. If you've decided to stay in your PhD program, even though you know you would rather be doing something else, and that feeling about doing something else doesn't go away, then it's time to ask yourself whether it's still worth "sticking it out."

The sunk cost fallacy also reflects a situation where how you think you should feel (e.g., I should feel happy about or grateful for doing this prestigious degree) is at odds with how you really feel (e.g., I really don't want to be here). You remain loyal to your own initiative, and you work hard to finish your degree, even as you cope with guilt for how you feel and with fear of the possibility of being shamed if you recognize and openly express your true feelings.

Fighting the sunken cost fallacy means returning to your values and goals rather than sinking into feelings of guilt. While you can't entirely ignore your emotions – and indeed, you should not – you can make an informed decision if you recognize that your emotions may be leading you to do something ultimately not in your best interest. Tap into your network to help you work through your emotions and move forward.

Is It Time to Leave?

For some students, the decision to leave a PhD program is a choice they may make or may be forced to make. If the program doesn't feel right, for whatever reason, and your heart is not in it, even after exploring the parameters of burnout and empathic strain, and consider answering the following questions:

- Do your values still resonate with you?
- Are there activities in each domain that reflect how you're practising your values? Remember, values are activated through your behaviours.
- How confident are you feeling about achieving your goals?
- Who among your people can you connect with to discuss your achievements? Seek their perspective on how far you've come and where you might go next.
- What skills have you developed? What skills have you enhanced? Have you forgotten to add a skill to your list of goals in any domain?
- Is there a lack of connection between your values and goals?
- Is there a disconnect between your intentions for your PhD and the bigger picture of your life?

Exploring Your Options

Take a look at your universe of possibilities and reflect on these questions before exploring your options: Do you see evidence of a lack of connection between your values and the content of your domains (i.e., the activities, people, and goals)? Can you strengthen the connection among these elements with the help of your people? Or would correcting the lack of connection require more time, money, and people than you have at this time? Would you consider a leave of absence, or is it worth withdrawing from your program?

Knowing your options, with or without a PhD, is crucial to your well-being. The sooner you gain a sense of what is possible, with the assistance of your network, the better. Not completing a PhD is not a failure. Not finishing what you started is not a failure. This is true whether you stop because of lack of funds or for another reason. There is life beyond a PhD. A professional counsellor or a career coach who caters to PhD students and graduates can help you find a life outside of academia. There should be no guilt or shame in leaving a PhD program, especially when that decision will allow you to flourish.

Coping with the End
The end of the PhD is like the denouement of a story, when you not only find out what happens but also how all the different threads are resolved. For some, the end of the journey can result in a joyous feeling of accomplishment and wonderment that never really ends. For others, finishing a PhD can feel like coming down to earth, not light as a feather but with a crash.

My experience leading up to my defence was one of frustration mixed with anxiety as I struggled with revising my dissertation and miscommunications with my supervisor about the timing of my defence. Even after the defence, I experienced insomnia as I made minor revisions before officially submitting my dissertation. In fact, I cried from relief and emotional exhaustion at the end. I remember travelling back home to visit with my sister and mother for a weekend to feel grounded again.

For those who experience it, this feeling of loss or grief is known as the postdefence comedown. It's a form of situational depression that some students develop. My supervisory team and mentors never mentioned it to me. One mentor said finishing their defence was "sweeter than cake." Another said I'd feel "lighter than air." But no one told me that after an initial high I might feel like I'd fallen off the edge of a cliff with a potentially hard landing. They didn't tell me I might need time to recuperate and regenerate.

In May 2007, three months after defending my dissertation, I travelled from Toronto to New Orleans with urban planners, community activists, and academics from the Planners Network (PN). PN is a group that values anti-oppression and social-justice approaches to planning. We gathered in New Orleans to learn from community members and residents of the city's Ninth Ward about their experiences recovering from Hurricane Katrina. What would they need from planners and researchers to help them to thrive? Leaders from faith communities and service organizations exposed me to a reality outside my own experiences and offered a counterbalance to my preoccupation with job hunting. I was reminded of my values of benevolence and social justice and how they are practised in everyday acts of kindness and mutual support. I experienced joy in seeing people rebuild their connections with family and new allies, and this helped me work through leftover feelings of anger and frustration from my PhD defence and my struggles on the job market. Returning to what matters most to me helped me move forward.

Although a postdoctoral fellowship put me on yet another learning curve, by the time I became a tenure-track professor, I had worked through my frustrations. I chose to explore the academic culture of my university to learn what was expected of me and what I wanted out of this new experience.

Still, I wish I'd been told about the complexity of the emotions I'd feel as a PhD student – a mixture of sweetness, joy, frustration, and grief. My experiences led me to conclude that academics don't discuss the emotional aspects of our PhD journeys enough, which ultimately makes it harder for students to do so. When I began working with graduate students, we never talked about the grief we felt whenever something ended and we had to start all over again. While I witnessed their disappointment and grief, I don't think I ever acknowledged it or their fear. I regret not sharing my own experience so they'd know that I understood how complex emotions can feel while pursuing and completing a doctoral degree.

✽ ✽ ✽

Throughout your PhD journey, seek out people from your inner, middle, and outer spheres with whom you can express and process emotions. If we all move through the tunnel of emotions into the light and encourage our peers to do the same, we can collectively transform academia into a place that supports connection and vitality. My hope is that your supervisor approaches naming, expressing, validating, and processing emotions with openness and compassion. Their positive engagement will also facilitate systemic change.

There is no cookie-cutter way to prepare for the post-PhD comedown. You might feel relief, happiness, and loss all at once, and that's okay. Seek the help you need to work through the last phase of your PhD and be kind to yourself.

Map It
Review the map of your universe of possibilities. Reflect on how your values have changed or shifted in priority since you started your PhD. What activities can you undertake or continue to practise to keep your values at the centre of the next phase of your journey, post-PhD?

Is there at least one activity in each domain that supports your overall wellness? If not, what can you do to facilitate wellness in your learning and research space? Are there activities outside of your PhD that could support your wellness? Have you included at least one or two activities that connect you with your PhD peers and with others who can sustain your sense of well-being?

Are there other skills on your skills inventory (Table 1, pages 37–40) related to self-care that you can enhance or learn? If so, do you need to modify one or more of your goals? Take another look at the list of resources you jotted down on page 61 in Chapter 3, and in the bottom right-hand corner of your universe of possibilities (pages 2–3). Are there services and resources you can add that would facilitate "feeling all the feels" and working through them? Finally, look at the list of people you created in Chapter 4 (page 75), and the network you created in Chapter 5 (page 91). Is there someone from your inner or middle circle – someone you might call an ally or mentor – who supports your engagement in personal or collective wellness?

Defining Success on Your Own Terms

EVERY LEARNING EXPERIENCE and connection with others can offer insight into what you might want for yourself and your future. Linking your values to your goals and reassessing them at each career stage will help you discover or choose your path and define success on your own terms. I learned this over the course of my career. When I was a student, it was sometimes hard to determine what success meant to me and to separate what it meant to me from what others (e.g., my family of origin, teachers, supervisor, and fellow students) expected of me. I was the product of the universe I inhabited and the constellations of people in my life. This has not changed. But I've learned more about what makes me tick and about the life I want to create for myself. I've learned to explore what success means to me.

Charting My Own Path

Two months after my defence, I travelled to San Francisco to attend the American Association of Geographers' annual conference. It would be the first time I'd present my dissertation research since my defence. Convocation was still two months away, but I could at least start calling myself a PhD. After a long day of conference sessions, my mentor invited me to go out for dinner with three other professors. Over the course of the meal, one of the professors talked passionately about their backyard renovations and customized deck furniture. They said it would cost at least twenty thousand dollars and add to the value of their home. As the lone PhD student at the table, I compared myself to the well-heeled professors and thought twenty thousand was a lot of money. I couldn't contribute much to the conversation because I knew nothing about home renovations.

As though they could read my mind, another professor changed the topic and asked me the question I was hoping to avoid all evening. What are your plans post-graduation? I responded optimistically. I told them I'd applied for a postdoctoral fellowship with government funding and that, knowing how stiff the competition would be, I had several backup plans. My backup plans included applying for any or all of the following: a university's in-house postdoctoral fellowship; two academic positions (one in the United States and one in Canada); a limited-term academic position; and an unpaid visiting-scholar position with terrific networking opportunities. If I got the latter, I'd supplement it with one or two paid teaching gigs, both of which involved job applications but because of their location had the added perk of plenty of visits with extended family. I might even have rattled off the list in one breath, as I was anticipating the question, and I was nervous. Given my tendency at the time to overshare, I told them I would apply for academic positions for two years, and if I was unsuccessful, I'd return to the public sector, where I still had strong contacts in my network.

My response was satisfactory, if not confident, which I ascertained when my mentor gave me a smile and a nod of reassurance. The waiter brought out the desserts, my favourite, crème brûlée. As I started the ritual of breaking through the sugary glass top to get to the creaminess beneath, Professor Deck piped up. They speculated that I wouldn't get the postdoc. The "letters for winners" had gone out two weeks ago, so if I hadn't heard, I should assume I was unsuccessful.

My heart beat fast. From the tone of the conversation, I worried it would shift into an interrogation. Before any further questions were posed or critiques were made about my future, I tried to shift course.

I told them our conversation was distracting me from my dessert. I suggested we stop the shop talk and focus on eating. Unfortunately, Professor Deck didn't listen to me. They were determined to find out more and asked me why returning to public service was among my plans. Before I could formulate my answer, they added that they believed a job in public service would prove to be disappointing. As far as I knew, none of the professors at my table had ever worked for the government. I tried to disregard Professor Deck's statement, but I started to regret sharing my plans and joining the professors for dinner.

I quietly set my dessert spoon on the dish but metal met ceramic – like the sound of my anger meeting my fragile anxiety. I said to Professor Deck, "You are making me feel uncomfortable. Please stop." Looking back, I know I treated my mentor and the other professors with respect. I could have laid out my boundaries more clearly, but I don't think Professor Deck would have respected them. Even as I declared what I wanted and tried not to make a scene, Professor Deck continued to make a meal out of me and my backup plans. Feeling exhausted and vulnerable, I started to weep, uncontrollably, all over my uneaten dessert. I handed money to my mentor to cover my bill and left the restaurant. I walked alone to my hotel and arrived at an empty room. My roommates had not yet returned from their night out on the town. I cried myself to sleep.

The next morning, I didn't feel like going to conference sessions. I decided to take my puffy-faced self for a ride on the Hyde Street cable car to Fisherman's Wharf, for a better view of the Golden Gate Bridge and, more importantly, for the Ghirardelli Chocolate Experience. Up we went on the cable car through historical neighbourhoods with beautiful architecture. I felt like a kid, just enjoying the ride, the sights, the sun, and the breeze. Light and joy were finding their way to me. When we arrived at Fisherman's Wharf, I got off the cable car and bought some chocolate. I took only a moment to look at the iconic bridge. I hopped back on the cable car for the ride back to the hotel.

As the cable car jostled, I realize I wanted to escape my reality. I felt sad. When we arrived at my stop, my heart was heavy. I was not ready to get off. I rode the cable car to the end, waited for it to turn around, and rode it all the way back to the wharf.

The operator noticed I had remained and struck up a conversation. They asked if I was a cable car fan. I told them I was loving the ride and confessed I didn't want to go back to the conference I was attending, at least not yet. They asked me why. I told them about my experience from the night before, that I was feeling beaten and needed to remind myself why I was there. When we reached Fisherman's Wharf, I didn't get off and readied myself to pay again. The operator said "no charge." They suggested I get off and check out the view, maybe for a bit longer this time. "Maybe, on the ride back, you'll figure out what you need to do." They promised to ring the bell when it was time to leave.

After enjoying the view of the Golden Gate Bridge one last time, I boarded the cable car. On the ride back, I reflected again on what I wanted. I reminded myself that even if I didn't get the postdoctoral fellowship, I had many backup plans, and one of them would work out. If they didn't, then I'd still find my own way, because I always have. I started to find my resolve.

Life was feeling sweeter, especially after my third Ghirardelli caramel. I recalled that I'd been really looking forward to this conference at the tail end of my PhD journey. I'd already presented my paper and felt great about it (for once!). Before I disembarked, I thanked the cable car driver for their kindness. I could feel the weight of the gruelling experience of sixteen hours ago starting to lift, and I decided to attend a conference session that afternoon.

Working my way through the afternoon crowds, I found a seat between two strangers at a packed session. I listened intently and took the time to formulate a question. When my opportunity arrived, I stood up, boldly introduced myself to the room, and posed my question. Two of the panellists honoured me with answers. At the end of the session, as people started to leave the room, the fellow sitting behind me, who I was surprised to discover was a renowned geographer, tapped my elbow and said, "Good question!" While I don't remember my question, I still recall the boost of energy I felt receiving their compliment; it was enough to tip me in the direction of hope. So I approached another famous scholar at the session, who I knew was promoting their department's recently advertised postdoctoral fellowship opportunity. I introduced myself, and they encouraged me to apply. I left the session feeling exhausted and exhilarated.

In retrospect, I managed to do more in that one conference session than I thought I could: to be present, to ask questions, to engage in conversation that might lead to a job, and to build up enough hopefulness to connect with others. I was getting back to what mattered most to me. I had returned to the conference space with a renewed sense of what I wanted and belief in myself.

I did not get the postdoctoral fellowship, but I did get an interview for a limited-term appointment to teach. I applied for the in-house university postdoctoral fellowship after deciding not to apply for tenure-track jobs in places where I didn't want to live. I knew my chances of being considered for a tenure-track job would improve once I finished publishing articles from my dissertation. I ended up turning down the limited-term position and was offered a postdoctoral fellowship at Queen's University, which I accepted. The fellowship enabled me to turn chapters of my dissertation into journal articles, start a new research project with a small grant, and teach undergraduate courses. Although the fellowship mirrored the experience of an assistant professorship, I received far less pay and had no benefits because postdocs were not unionized at Queen's at that time. Yet, back then, as now, I was committed to defining what success meant to me, on my own terms. Every little effort in my own interest would breed success. Eventually, I ended up applying for, and getting, a tenure-track assistant professor position at Queen's University – the same spot where I was doing my fellowship – and I stayed there until I shifted course again and chose self-employment, launching Viswali Consulting at the end of 2019.

The Downside of "Fake It 'Til You Make It"

When I first started the tenure-track position, I asked a visiting professor who I admired whether they had a secret to succeeding in academia. I had always admired their wit, their ability to navigate academia and call out racism through their research. Their answer to my question was "fake it 'til you make it!" I've thought about their answer since. What does "making it" really mean, and according to whose measure? Does faking it until you succeed mean ignoring what you value most, or does it mean focusing more on performance and appearance than what matters most to you? I've embraced the notion that I'm a "space invader," a term coined by Nirmal Puwar to refer to a person who inhabits spaces not intended for them. Did my false bravado constitute "faking it"?

Throughout your PhD journey and beyond, whether you remain in academia or build a career outside of it, you'll consider what others think of you in relation to what you think of yourself and where you think you should be versus where you are. If you're from an equity-deserving group, then you might grapple with appreciating the university environment while negotiating with it. Faking it is not a reality for people whose abilities and attributes stand out and may not be recognized as strengths, beyond so-called celebrations of "difference" by institutions, including universities. The downside of faking it is that each person faces different risks in bringing their authentic self. Being authentic is not something that people with histories of being marginalized can do readily – not without the risk of being stereotyped or excluded further. "Making it" depends on what "achievement" and "success" mean to you. Faking courage for too long prevented me from seeing that my goals had veered far away from my values. I got back on course by embracing my vulnerability as my strength and caring less about what others thought about me. Showing my vulnerability, including choosing who I shared my feelings and stories with, allowed me to better manage the risks.

Achieving milestones will be important to your supervisors and the university. Milestones let them know you're moving through the system, according to their timelines. However, milestones can also be a way for you to gauge where you are; they provide you with opportunities to consider what support or insights you need at various stages. Milestones set by the university will be important to you, but don't forget how your goals relate to your domains and, ultimately, your values. It will be harder for you to fool yourself or claim false bravado when you're setting your own milestones and the terms of your own success too.

Appraise before You Strategize

As a student, putting work into building your network will help you appraise your values before you strategize about what comes next after you complete your degree or leave your program. You might have your eye on a tenure-track job. But then again, you might want to keep your options open and have backup plans that could become your primary choice outside of academia. Or maybe your Plan A is a job outside of academia, and your Plan B is a combination of options in or outside academia. If I didn't get a tenure-track job within two years, my Plan B was pursuing a combination of public sector research and policy jobs with teaching on the side.

While most PhD students will not get jobs as tenure-track professors, you may still want an academic position, because that's what PhD programs train and expect students to desire and achieve. As noted in the Council of Canadian Academies' 2021 report *Degrees of Success*, students who choose not to pursue a career in academia are too often made to feel ashamed about their choices, especially by peers who see a nonacademic job as "less than" being a professor. Don't fall prey to the falsehood that the jobs outside of academia available to PhD holders don't pay as well or offer as much prestige. It's deeply discouraging to think that PhD students are being made to feel ashamed for pursuing success on their own terms and outside academia. Life is yours to live.

In my experience in the social sciences, third year was a turning point after all the coursework and comprehensive exams were done.

Students launch into their research seriously and whole-heartedly, and they start to consider where they're at and where they want to be after they graduate. It's also a time when discussions about funding a PhD might turn into discussions about financing it, especially if funding is running out.

Planning strategically is mostly goal-oriented and can keep you focused on tasks and timelines, but if your plans are not linked to your values, you might lose touch with the overall purpose of your doctorate. Use your universe of possibilities to consider how your goals link to your activities. Review your skills inventory in Chapter 2. How important are your skills now? What skills do you need to enter the next year of your PhD or to prepare for a future job? Consider trying out the individual development plans and charts offered by your university and, if necessary, modify them deliberately to suit your intentions. Alternatively, consider working with a career coach to prepare for and plot out your next steps.

Looking back now at my experience with Professor Deck, I took weeks following the conference to work through the emotional leftovers. To this day, it's a watershed moment for me (and not just because of all the tears)! I worked through my emotions and connected with people who knew me. People from my network helped me see my universe of possibilities and supplemented my resolve. I believe success is based on factors you set for yourself, and your network is crucial in navigating your universe of possibilities.

In *The Science of Science*, Dashun Wang and Albert-László Barabási argue that networks are the key predictor of success, judging by the buzz that a person or a person's body of work, or a single piece of work (i.e., research, art, or performance), generates. Your success will be based on what a community notices about the piece you produce or perform and whether it is rewarded in the days, months, or decades after it's launched and shared in the public domain. Your network can be powerful because of how people connect to you and to one another and what you can do together. However, it's your agency and appreciation of what matters that will make your career, and the rest of your life, meaningful.

I define success on my own terms. I recognize my approach may go against Wang and Barabási's that success is determined by one's network. I can't deny that success is a social phenomenon. My social interaction with Professor Deck shows that defying the so-called best intentions of people within my academic community was often challenging, emotionally and mentally.

❊ ❊ ❊

Knowing your unique combination of skills and experience will help you connect with others and give you insight into what makes you stand out. Go back to your skills inventory and your lists of goals, activities, and people in your network. Talk with your people and ask them what they think makes you unique. Why do they think people should be connecting with you, and you with them? You may learn, through their stories, what they think is feeding your success now and what will fuel it in the near future or over the long term. Consider their feedback as you formulate what success looks like for you. Remember that these conversations are meant to inform, not determine, how you understand success. You determine what success means to you.

Life's unfolding reveals a universe of possibilities over time, so what success means to you could change. Success should not be determined by what society defines as success. If that were the case, I believe I would not flourish. I'd simply be surviving in the human shell that people see while my spirit slowly disintegrates. Being deliberate about my choices, aware of constraints, and open to opportunities in my universe of possibilities helps me thrive. Keeping my goals and values aligned is a work in progress.

Map It

Before you strategize about the trajectory of your PhD, appraise your values and goals. Take another look at your values: do you need to reprioritize them? If so, consider redoing the values assessment in Chapter 1. It will ensure that you have your values prioritized, that they make sense to you, and that you can develop goals that align with your values. The map of your universe of possibilities will help you keep your values at the core of your PhD journey.

Take a look at your domains. Do they reflect where you are in your studies? Do you need to modify the domains? For example, do you still have coursework as a domain, even though you have completed your courses? Do you need to change a domain to better reflect where you want to be next, whether it's job hunting, conference planning, or networking?

Take a look at your goals. Are you eager to turn your informal goals into measurable ones, using the SMART system? Do you have at least one skill to develop or enhance within each domain? The people you list – your allies, mentors, and sponsors – are the people to whom you'll be accountable when it comes to your goals. Is your supervisor your ally, or do they already occupy the position of mentor or sponsor? Are there people in your middle or outer network who can help you build new skills or enhance existing skills? Are they listed under "My People"?

As a final step, in the figure below, list the keywords that you would use to describe success in your own terms. Or maybe you would rather create a sentence that describes what success looks like to you. Once you have your words or sentence, add them to your universe of possibilities.

What Success Means to Me

Each chapter in this book encourages you to reflect on and connect with ideas and people so you can identify the key components of your map of possibilities. Take a moment to appreciate all the components and the connections among them. Are there additional changes that you need to make? Can you see important connections among your domains, your goals, your activities, your people, and the resources that keep you curious and that help you meet your stay true to your values?

Conclusion

Living Your Values

THROUGHOUT *The Deliberate Doctorate*, I emphasize that your values can inform every aspect of your PhD journey. But don't hold them too tightly; they are a compass to guide you through the hard work in different domains of your PhD. Your values will remind you when you're on track, when you're not, and when you may need to recalibrate. I've invited you to consider how you can align your values with your goals to connect and network with the people who can support you. I encourage you to work through the complex emotions you'll experience, sometimes a mixture of eager anticipation and fear, as you map your journey and define success in your own terms. My hope is that, in being deliberate, your values will be your touchstone as you undertake your doctorate and plan your future.

The mapping exercises, which place values at the centre, will help you envisage what is possible at each stage of your journey. It's *your* map first; something for people to influence second. Use your map as a guide for strategic planning; it will help you appraise your values before you strategize about university milestones and endpoints, such as a job or a career path.

Values challenge the pragmatic processes of academic culture in ways that goals do not. Goal setting falls into the prescriptive approach of checking boxes, which can be challenging, especially when government funders ask universities to measure outputs (i.e., the number of graduates) and inputs (i.e., the number of students entering and retained by a university) each year. However, values are too rarely incorporated into the process of individual academic goal setting, leaving students with little guidance on how to discover their values and assess how they're relevant to their PhD. Values and goals, when aligned, are powerful.

The complex emotions that accompany the PhD journey need to be acknowledged. PhD students work and build relationships with allies and mentors in universities. Academic culture plays a role in sculpting the values of graduate students. When students are pressured to conform to academic culture, morals – in the form of rules that contain "should," "must," and "required" as keywords – too often replace values. If your values don't align with the academy, beyond the values of academic achievement and skills attainment, you may experience moral distress. Your encounters with structural barriers may become a fundamental obstacle to your success. This is when knowing what you want, what you don't want, and what you're willing to do and for how long come into play. A values-focused journey to earning a PhD will be more likely if your university supports your approach as much as it supports you in achieving your degree milestones.

Some argue that we can't discover our purpose; we must choose it. But I think purpose is determined by curiosity and choice. Some of us grow up with few choices or no understanding that we have choices to make. So we choose what is evident or available. Others grow up believing they can choose from a bounty of options. Still others experience a combination of the two. Pragmatism reigns as I work with what I have available to me, and because of my aspirations and my privilege, I create or investigate all options and seek access to resources to deliberately fulfill my purpose in this world. Granted, I'm a work in progress, but my path has been clearer since I began prioritizing my values and aligning them with my goals. While my values are consistently present, my goals have changed and will likely change again.

Conclusion

My PhD journey defined an important part of my life, and it continues to shape the life I've chosen. I hope my stories give you insight into some of the imperfections of the doctoral experience and the benefits of doing a PhD because you want to, and not simply because it's something you should do for someone else or for a job that may not be guaranteed. I've tried to be pragmatic about the challenges you may face.

Perhaps after exploring the exercises and ideas in this book, you've decided that a PhD is not for you. If that's the case, then the time you've taken to reflect, connect, and act was well spent. Live your values and feed your curiosity by taking a different path to a fulfilling life. For those of you who plan to continue on your journey to your PhD, deliberate doctorates are needed in every sector of society. You can contribute your skills, knowledge, and experience to problem solving in many ways and places. Academia does not need to be your home base.

Be deliberate in living your values as best you can, so that no matter where you land, you'll always bring purpose and meaning to your life.

Further Reading

Introduction: Being Deliberate

Brown, Gavin, ed. *How to Get Your PhD: A Handbook for the Journey.* Oxford: Oxford University Press, 2021. **In most of the case examples, this book foregrounds the STEM context.**

Calarco, Jessica McCrory. *A Field Guild to Grad School: Uncovering the Hidden Curriculum.* Princeton, NJ: Princeton University Press, 2020. **Chapter 1 provides an overview of the stages of the PhD in the context of US-based universities.**

Rugg, Gordon, and Marian Petre. *The Unwritten Rules of PhD Research.* 3rd ed. London: Open University Press, 2020. **Chapter 2, "The Many Shapes of the PhD," provides an overview of the phases of the doctoral process and related terminology in the context of universities in the United Kingdom.**

Sverdlik, Anna, and Nathan C. Hall. "Not Just a Phase: Exploring the Role of Program Stage on Well-Being and Motivation in Doctoral Students." *Journal of Adult and Continuing Education* 26, 1 (2020): 97–104. https://doi.org/10.1177/1477971419842887. **This article looks at phases of the PhD in the Canadian context and how the socialization and well-being of doctoral students affects their motivation in each stage.**

Chapter 1: Discovering Your Values

Ahmed, Sarah. *Living A Feminist Life.* Durham, NC: Duke University Press, 2017.

Harper, Faith G. *Unf°ck Your Boundaries: Build Better Relationships through Consent, Communication, and Expressing Your Needs.* Portland,

OR: Microcosm, 2020. **A no-nonsense exploration of why societal and systemic boundaries are hard for many people to set. It offers an approach for exploring different types of boundaries; personal reactions to setting and keeping boundaries; and ways to communicate boundaries, seek consent, and hold oneself and others accountable.**

Harris, Russ. *ACT Made Simple*. 2nd ed. Oakland, CA: New Harbinger, 2019. **Chapter 9 provides important insights into the quality of values, how they differ from goals, and how to work with them. Page 220 offers a "Summary of Common Values Techniques."**

hooks, bell. "A Revolution of Values: The Promise of Multi-cultural Change." "Cultural Diversity," special issue, *Journal of the Midwest Modern Language Association* 26, 1 (1993): 4–11. **The quotation is taken from page 6.**

Katherine, Anne. *Boundaries: Where You End and I Begin*. New York: Simon and Schuster, 1991.

Kendal, Dave, and Christopher M. Raymond. "Understanding Pathways to Shifting People's Values Over Time in the Context of Social-Ecological Systems." *Sustainability Science* 14 (2019): 1333–42. https://doi.org/10.1007/s11625-018-0648-0.

Life Values Inventory. "Life Values Inventory: Values Identification Program." https://www.lifevaluesinventory.org/. **This is my favourite free values inventory; it helps prioritize your values and encourages reflection on the behaviours that might support them.**

Chapter 2: Setting Goals Aligned with Your Values
Beyond the Professoriate. "10 Transferable Skills from Your PhD That Employers Want." https://beyondprof.com/10-transferable-skills-from-your-phd-that-employers-want/.

Bolles, Richard. *What Color Is Your Parachute? A Practical Manual for Job-Hunters and Career-Changers*. New York: Ten Speed Press, 2022. **With a new edition every few years, this book has been a favourite for decades. It addresses everything from developing a rigorous self-inventory, including skills identification, to preparing for informational interviews and the job hunt.**

Conklin, James. *Balancing Acts: A Human Systems Approach to Organizational Change*. Toronto: Rotman/University of Toronto Press, 2021.

Harris, Russ. *ACT Made Simple*. 2nd ed. Oakland, CA: New Harbinger, 2019. **Chapter 21 explores the importance of committed action to meeting goals and the application of SMART goals.**

Locke, Edwin A., and Gary P. Latham. "Building a Practically Useful Theory of Goal Setting and Task Motivation: A 35-Year Odyssey." *American Psychologist* 57, 9 (2002): 705–17.

University of Michigan, Student Life, University Career Center. "PhD Transferable Skills." https://careercenter.umich.edu/article/phd-transferable-skills.

Chapter 3: Making the Most of Your PhD Supervisor

Clow, Erin. "Choosing a Graduate Program Supervisor." *University Affairs*, March 15, 2016. https://www.universityaffairs.ca/career-advice/career-advice-article/choosing-a-graduate-program-supervisor/.

Columbia University. "The Definitive 'What Do I Ask/Look For' in a PhD Advisor Guide." https://www.cs.columbia.edu/wp-content/uploads/2019/03/Get-Advisor.pdf.

Gibbs, Kenneth D., and Kimberley A. Griffin. "What Do I Want to Be with My PhD? The Roles of Personal Values and Structural Dynamics in Shaping the Career Interests of Recent Biomedical Science PhD Graduates." *Life Sciences Education*, 12, 4 (2017): 711–23. https://www.lifescied.org/doi/10.1187/cbe.13-02-0021.

Henry, Frances, Enakshi Dua, Carl E. James, Audrey Kobayashi, Peter Li, Howard Ramos, and Malinda S. Smith. *The Equity Myth: Racialization and Indigeneity at Canadian Universities*. Vancouver: UBC Press, 2017.

Kirchherr, Julian. *The Lean PhD: Radically Improve the Efficiency, Quality and Impact of Your Research*. London: Red Globe Press, 2018.

Rugg, Gordon, and Marian Petre. *The Unwritten Rules of PhD Research*. 3rd ed. London: Open University Press, 2020. **Chapter 2, "The Many Shapes of the PhD," provides an overview of the phases of the doctoral process and related terminology in the context of universities in the United Kingdom. The quotation is taken from page 46.**

Saló-Salgado, Lluís, Angi Acocella, Ignacio Arzuaga García, Souha
El Mousadik, and Augustine Zvinavashe. "Managing Up: How to
Communicate Effectively with Your PhD Adviser." *Nature*, December
10, 2021. https://doi.org/10.1038/d41586-021-03703-z.

Sousa, Bailey, and Alexander Clark. "How Academics Can Handle
Conflict Better." *University Affairs*, August 29, 2022. https://www.
universityaffairs.ca/career-advice/effective-successfull-happy-academic/
how-academics-can-handle-conflict-better/.

University of British Columbia, Graduate and Postdoctoral Studies.
"Supervisor Expectations." https://www.grad.ubc.ca/handbook-graduate-
supervision/supervisor-expectations. **This website has a downloadable
supervisor-student agreement that lists expectations that can be
reviewed and discussed between student and supervisor.**

University of Waterloo, School of Public Health Sciences.
"Topics to Discuss with Your Potential Supervisor." https://
uwaterloo.ca/public-health-sciences/future-graduate-students/
topics-discuss-your-potential-supervisor.

Chapter 4: Assembling Your Supervisory Team

Cabral, Amber. *Allies and Advocates: Creating an Inclusive and Equitable
Culture.* Hoboken, NJ: John Wiley and Sons, 2021.

Calarco, Jessica McCrory. *A Field Guild to Grad School: Uncovering the
Hidden Curriculum.* Princeton, NJ: Princeton University Press, 2020.
**Chapter 2, "Building Your Team," offers resources and information
useful for graduate students in the United States.**

Hewlett, Sylvia Ann. *Forget a Mentor, Find a Sponsor: The New Way to
Fast-Track Your Career.* Boston, MA: Harvard Business Review Press,
2013.

–. *The Sponsor Effect: How to Be a Better Leader by Investing in Others.*
Boston, MA: Harvard Business Review Press, 2019.

Weber, Jeff. "The Roles of Allies, Mentors and Sponsors in Employee
Development." *Forbes*, September 27, 2019. https://www.forbes.com/
sites/forbeshumanresourcescouncil/2019/09/27/the-roles-of-allies-
mentors-and-sponsors-in-employee-development/?sh=49b304ad38ee.

Further Reading

Chapter 5: Networking without Feeling Smarmy about It

Academic Designer. "Social Media Platforms for Academics: A Breakdown of the Networks," August 9, 2019. https://theacademicdesigner.com/2019/social-media-platforms/. **This website includes information on managing social media, dealing with negative reactions, and using direct messages to communicate with academics.**

Beyond the Professoriate. "Academic Networking for PhD Students: 5 Ways to Do It Better." https://beyondprof.com/networking-for-phd-students/.

Goldfarb, Anna. "Should You Send That DM? Well ..." *New York Times,* December 10, 2019. https://www.nytimes.com/2019/12/10/smarter-living/how-to-send-a-direct-message.html.

Kang, Sonia K., Katherine A. DeCelles, András Tilcsik, and Sora Jun. "Whitened Résumés: Race and Self-Presentation in the Labor Market." *Administrative Science Quarterly* 61, 3 (2016): 469–50. https://tspace.library.utoronto.ca/bitstream/1807/72386/1/KangDecellesTilcsikJun2016ASQ.pdf.

Minocha, Shailey, and Marian Petre. *Handbook for Social Media for Researchers and Supervisors: Digital Technologies for Research Dialogues.* Milton Keynes, UK: The Open University/Vitae, 2012. https://www.vitae.ac.uk/vitae-publications/reports/innovate-open-university-social-media-handbook-vitae-2012.pdf.

Oreopoulos, Philip. "Why Do Skilled Immigrants Struggle in the Labor Market? A Field Experiment with Thirteen Thousand Resumes." *American Economic Journal: Economic Policy* 3, 4 (2011): 148–71. https://doi.org/10.1257/pol.3.4.148.

University of California, Berkeley. Career Center. "Informational Interviewing." https://career.berkeley.edu/start-exploring/informational-interviews/.

Wenger, Etienne C., and William M. Snyder. "Communities of Practice: The Organizational Frontier." *Harvard Business Review* 78, 1 (2000): 139–45.

Wenger-Trayner, Etienne, and Beverly Wenger-Trayner. "Communities of Practice: A Brief Overview of the Concept and Its Uses." Wenger-Trayner.com, April 15, 2015. https://wenger-trayner.com/introduction-to-communities-of-practice/.

"What Is Networking, with Jennifer Polk." *YouTube*, August 12, 2021. https://www.youtube.com/watch?v=didV0bHHsGs.

Chapter 6: "Feeling All the Feels" through Your PhD

Beasy, Kim, Sherridan Emery, and Joseph Crawford. "Drowning in the Shallows: An Australian Study of the PhD Experience of Wellbeing." *Teaching in Higher Education* 26, 4 (2021): 602–18. https://www.tandfonline.com/doi/full/10.1080/13562517.2019.1669014.

Brown, Brené. *Atlas of the Heart: Mapping Meaningful Connection and the Language of Human Experience*. New York: Random House, 2021.

Burke, Tarana, and Brené Brown, eds. *You Are Your Best Thing: Vulnerability, Shame Resilience, and the Black Experience – An Anthology*. New York: Random House, 2021.

Clance, Pauline Rose, and Suzanne Ament Imes. "The Imposter Phenomenon in High Achieving Women: Dynamics and Therapeutic Intervention." *Psychotherapy: Theory, Research and Practice* 15, 3 (1978): 241–47. https://doi.org/10.1037/h0086006.

Ginwright, Shawn A. "The Blues of Vulnerability: Love and Healing Black Youth." In Burke and Brown, *You Are Your Best Thing*, 98–108. **The quotation is taken from page 107.**

Katherine, Anne. *Boundaries: Where You End and I Begin*. New York: Simon Schuster, 1991.

Jones, Angel M. "Coping with Postdefense Depression." *Inside Higher Ed*, May 12, 2021. https://www.insidehighered.com/advice/2021/05/13/dealing-mixed-emotions-completing-your-phd-opinion.

Lambie, Glenn W., and Nicole Vaccaro. "Doctoral Counselor Education Students' Levels of Research Self-Efficacy, Perceptions of the Research Training Environment, and Interest in Research." *Counselor Education and Supervision* 50, 4 (2011): 243–58. https://doi.org/10.1002/j.1556-6978.2011.tb00122.x.

Lovitts, Barbara E. "The Transition to Independent Research: Who Makes It, Who Doesn't, and Why." *Journal of Higher Education* 79, 3 (2008): 296–325. https://doi.org/10.1353/jhe.0.0006.

Further Reading

Manly, Carla Marie. *Joy from Fear: Create the Life of Your Dreams by Making Fear Your Friend*. New York: Familius LLC, 2019. **This book argues that fear can be a great learning tool for self-knowledge.**

Maté, Gabor. *When the Body Says No: The Cost of Hidden Stress*. Toronto: Vintage Canada, 2003.

Mathieu, Françoise. *The Compassion Fatigue Workbook: Creative Tools for Transforming Compassion Fatigue and Vicarious Traumatization*. London: Routledge, 2011. **An excellent workbook to explore and address, both individually and collectively, the symptoms of empathic strain, referred to as "compassion fatigue." The quotation is taken from page 8.**

Nagoski, Emily, and Amelia Nagoski. *Burnout: The Secret to Unlocking the Stress Cycle*. New York: Ballantine, 2020. **A detailed exploration of burnout, its effect on women, and ways to manage, if not stop, the stress cycle.**

Petersen, Anne Helen. *Can't Even: How Millennials Became the Burnout Generation*. Boston: Houghton Mifflin Harcourt, 2020.

Raimondi, Thomas P. "Compassion Fatigue in Higher Education: Lessons from Other Helping Fields." *Change: The Magazine of Higher Learning* 51, 3 (2019): 52–58.https://doi.org/10.1080/00091383.2019.1606609.

Rosenberg, Marshall B. *Nonviolent Communication: A Language of Life*. 3rd ed. Encinitas, CA: Puddle Dancer Press, 2015. **The quotations are from pages 44–46.**

Selye, Hans. "The General Adaptation Syndrome and the Diseases of Adaptation." *Journal of Clinical Endocrinology and Metabolism* 6, 2 (1946): 117–230. https://doi.org/10.1210/jcem-6-2-117.

Stubb, J., K. Pyhältö, and K. Lonka. "Balancing between Inspiration and Exhaustion: PhD Students' Experienced Socio-psychological Well-Being." *Studies in Continuing Education* 33, 1 (2011): 33–50. https://doi.org/10.1080/0158037X.2010.515572.

Tulshyan, Ruchika, and Jodi-Anne Burey. "Stop Telling Women They Have Imposter Syndrome." *Harvard Business Review*, February 11, 2021. https://hbr.org/2021/02/stop-telling-women-they-have-imposter-syndrome.

van Dernoot Lipsky, Laura, with Connie Burk. *Trauma Stewardship: An Everyday Guide to Caring for Self while Caring for Others.* San Francisco, CA: Berrett-Koehler Publishers, 2009.

Warner, Mona L. *Ayurveda's Three Pillars of Health: A Map to Health, Resilience, and Well-Being.* Kingston, ON: Mona L. Warner/Archangel Ink, 2019.

Willcox, Gloria. "The Feeling Wheel: A Tool of Expanding Awareness of Emotions and Increasing Spontaneity and Intimacy." *Transactional Analysis Journal* 12, 4 (1982): 274–76. https://doi.org/10.1177/036215378201200411.

Woolston, Chris. "PhDs: The Torturous Truth." *Nature* 575 (2019): 403–6. https://www.nature.com/articles/d41586-019-03459-7.
This article presents the results of the 2019 PhD Survey.

World Health Organization. "Burn-Out an 'Occupational Phenomenon': International Classification of Diseases," departmental news, May 28, 2019. https://www.who.int/news/item/28–05–2019-burn-out-an-occupational-phenomenon-international-classification-of-diseases.

Chapter 7: Defining Success on Your Own Terms

Council of Canadian Academies. *Degrees of Success: The Expert Panel on the Labour Market Transition of PhD Graduates.* Ottawa: Council of Canadian Academies, 2021. https://www.cca-reports.ca/reports/the-labour-market-transition-of-phd-graduates/.

Clow, Erin. "Don't Make Me Feel Ashamed of My Career Aspirations." *University Affairs*, August 4, 2015. https://www.universityaffairs.ca/opinion/in-my-opinion/dont-make-me-feel-ashamed-of-my-career-aspirations/.

Maymon, Rebecca, Laura Nilson, and Claire Edrington. "Where Can a PhD in STEM Lead?" *University Affairs*, September 23, 2021. https://www.universityaffairs.ca/career-advice/career-advice-article/where-can-a-phd-in-stem-lead/.

Further Reading

Pero, Rebecca. "Why Grad Students Should Engage in Alternative, Non-academic Career Activities." *University Affairs*, September 27, 2016. https://www.universityaffairs.ca/career-advice/career-advice-article/grad-students-engage-alternative-non-academic-career-activities/.

Puwar, Nirmal. *Space Invaders: Race, Gender and Bodies Out of Place.* Oxford: Berg, 2004.

Queen's University, School of Graduate Studies and Postdoctoral Affairs. "Individual Development Plan (IDP)." https://www.queensu.ca/exph/idp. **A downloadable IDP workbook for students and a companion supervisor's guidebook. Look for similar information on your university's career, leadership, and graduate studies webpages.**

Talas, Annamaria, dir. *The Nature of Things.* Season 61, episode 14, "The Science of Success." Aired April 1, 2022. https://gem.cbc.ca/media/the-nature-of-things/s61e14?cmp=DM_DOCS_FEED_GEMCARD_the-science-of-success. **This episode explores Wang and Barabási's research on the relationship between networks and success.**

University of Minnesota, Graduate School, Individual Development Plan. "Network with the Individual Development Plan." https://grad.umn.edu/academic-career-support/individual-development-plan. **Real examples of individual development plans for PhD students and postdoctoral fellows at different stages of their careers. It includes a list of transferable skills for students on different career paths.**

Wang, Dashun, and Albert-László Barabási. *The Science of Science.* New York: Cambridge University Press, 2021. **Compelling research on how networks determine success in the sciences.**